SALEM COLLEGE
LIBRARY

The Archie K. Davis
Collection of
Southern History & Literature

Number Twenty-Nine:
THE WALTER PRESCOTT WEBB
MEMORIAL LECTURES

Southern Writers

AND THEIR WORLDS

Southern
AND THEIR WORLDS
Writers

by Christopher Morris, Susan A. Eacker,
Anne Goodwyn Jones, Bertram Wyatt-Brown,
and Charles Joyner

Introduction by Michael O'Brien

Edited by Christopher Morris and Steven G. Reinhardt

Published for the University of Texas at Arlington by
TEXAS A&M UNIVERSITY PRESS
College Station

The paper used in this book meets the minimum requirements
of the American National Standard for Permanence
of Paper for Printed Library Materials, Z39.48–1984.
Binding materials have been chosen for durability.
∞

Library of Congress Cataloging-in-Publication Data

Southern writers and their worlds / by Christopher Morris . . . [et al.]
; introduction, by Michael O'Brien ; edited by Christopher Morris
and Steven G. Reinhardt.—1st ed.
    p. cm.—(The Walter Prescott Webb memorial lectures ; no.
29)
Includes index.
ISBN 0-89096-692-3 (alk. paper)
    1. American literature—Southern States—History and criticism.
2. Southern States—In literature. I. Morris, Christopher
(Christopher Charles) II. Reinhardt, Steven G., 1949– .
III. Series: Walter Prescott Webb memorial lectures ; 29.
PS261.S615 1996
810.9′975—dc20   95-39356
                                       CIP

To Wendell Knox,

TEXAN AND SOUTHERNER

Contents

Preface

Once a year, the department of history of the University of Texas at Arlington invites several distinguished scholars to participate in the Walter Prescott Webb Memorial Lectures, an event that honors Texas' well-known historian of the West. Southern Writers and Their Worlds, the theme of the twenty-ninth annual lectures, may seem rather removed from the Great Plains of Texas that were so dear to Professor Webb. But, then, Texas belongs not just to the West; it also belongs to the South.

On behalf of the UTA history department, the editors would like to acknowledge several benefactors and friends of the Webb lectures. C. B. Smith, Sr., an Austin businessman and former student of Walter Prescott Webb, generously established the Webb Endowment Fund and made possible the publication of the lecture presentations. Jenkins and Virginia Garrett of Fort Worth have long shown both loyalty and generosity to UTA. Major support also came from the Rudolf Hermanns Endowment for the Liberal Arts. President Ryan Amacher supported our efforts by extending his warm hospitality to our guests, and department head Kenneth R. Philp offered invaluable guidance to planning the event. Thanks also to Philip Cohen, of the UTA department of English, who shared his insights during the judging of the essays submitted for the Webb-Smith Essay Competition.

We dedicate this volume to Wendell Knox, historian and teacher, Texan and Southerner, who retired after thirty years of valuable service.

Southern Writers

AND THEIR WORLDS

Introduction

MICHAEL O'BRIEN

For the study of the American South, its culture, and thought, we live in interesting times. The essays in this book, by offering a rich consistency of insights, are a case in point. It is shown how the dark levities of antebellum humor were driven, in part, by male anxieties about belonging to modernity's market economy. It is explained how Louisa McCord, at the same time, arrived at antifeminism by being painfully and intimately aware of the degrading inferiorities that society thrust upon women. It is indicated how the literature of the early twentieth century evidenced a moment of malleability in gender roles, when women were encouraged if thwarted, while men were confused and terrified by uncertainty. It is suggested how melancholy and neurosis have been knitted into the fabric of literary creativity, in the modern South and elsewhere. It is told how there developed a complicated controversy over William Styron's *The Confessions of Nat Turner*. These interpretations are offered by senior scholars such as Bertram Wyatt-Brown, Charles Joyner, and Anne Goodwyn Jones, whose gifts and accomplishments are deservedly well established, as well as by two younger historians, Susan Eacker and Christopher Morris, who here give promise of high distinction.

Having played no role in the planning or performance of the Webb lectures, I have read these essays as any reader might, finding interest as interest struck me.¹ I was most taken with tone and language. These phrases come from Eacker's essay: "inexplicably bound up," "conflicted authorship," "paradoxical role," "playfully sardonic," "a multitude of forms," "subtle acts of insurrection," "the restless mind," "unstable contours." These come from Morris: "Change . . . rapid . . . utterly mystifying," "very scary," "quick, jarring, and confusing," "male apprehension," "somewhat detached," "men. . . . have lost control over their lives." These from Jones: "Powerful and painful," "dissecting . . . lopping off . . . carve. . . . suture," "natural and unnatural," "a Procrustean bed," "disillusionments . . . massive and deep," "stunned," "floundered," "surrender and loss," "an air both of giddiness and of terror." From Wyatt-Brown: "Dread of shame and failure," "agony," "deep estrangement," "mourning, depression, and their sometime consort, mania," "self-destructive dictates," "guilt and grief," "inner doubts and confusions," "dangerous interior things." From Joyner: "Bleak and chill," "cold and musty," "shadowy paradoxical band," "visions of apocalypse," "guilt-stricken," "powerful but pathetic," "polarities of power and submission, of authority and subservience, of being and nothingness," "vain and delusive comfort," "symbolic ashes."

This grim language is not uniform. Morris has the lightest tone, as befits his subject, though the humor he studies is explained by anxiety. Eacker's manner is robust and convinced, but she invites us to respect a woman whose story speaks, partly of intellectual accomplishment, but also of sharp limitations and resignation. Jones writes with confidence of female advancement in the early twentieth century, but also, almost with pity, of the impotence this seems to have occasioned in Southern men, whose women had walked off their pedestals into gin houses. Wyatt-Brown is bleakest and seems to find no way for creativity to be released other than by an omnipresence of despair. Joyner is most eager to find a chink of light; he speaks of "the power of guilt and the possibility of redemption." He ends by hoping that "perhaps—in some strange, undefinable way, some way unfathomable by any ideology presently known, but in some way simply bestowed by the compassion of art—Nat Turner's symbolic ashes may yet give forth light." But guilt has "power," while redemption is only a "possibility"; light may come, but we have no ideology to generate it.

The South portrayed here is not a cheerful place but difficult, unresolved, and unresolvable. Why so bleak? The Southern tradition has seldom, it is true, been indifferent to the dark conclusion; the power of that impulse, mostly forced by the intractabilities of race, is now many generations past the savage executions of the Southampton Insurrection and does not seem to be flagging. But there is more at stake now, something newer. To the old warfare of race, our historians and literary critics have added the still more ancient warfare of gender, newly configured and placed to the fore. These are not peculiarly Southern problems, but American as well. No one seems to know what to do about race in America; most of the options seem to have been tried and found wanting. Now, also, we have grown conflicted on the great matter of feminism, of gender, of how men and women should act towards one another. The clear idea of our early feminism, the encouraging idea of equality, has been disintegrated into myriad distinctions, of practical difficulties, of faltering male egos, of female uncertainty about multiplying and exhausting roles, of angers barely controlled or released; we have only tattered road maps, scribbled on by many wearying travelers, to the future of gender. Much seems to fail.

Philosophically, in the wider world, there is confusion; we are deemed to stand at the end of things, poststructuralist, postmodernist, postindustrial, postfeminist. Our intellectual landscape is disfigured with the remains of what went before, the littered matériel of failed sallies and doomed expeditions: the rusting computers of cliometricians, the rotting court transcripts of new social historians, the torn poll data of new political historians, the confetti of doodles by new historicists. We are variously told that the center cannot hold, that our Israel can have no kings, that the world is only representation, that we fashion and manipulate the pattern of words and theory, that only self and its figurations can count.[2] Process alone exists.

It is a delicate question, whether and when an interest in process betrays vitality or not. There was vitality in the early years of Marxism and Freudianism, when methodologies were elaborated and narratives remade that in turn helped to remake our worlds. But enrapture with methodology can be evidence, not of vitality but of the death of curiosity about the world and the labor to which inquisitiveness gives rise. Such moments can come for many reasons, but one is when an intelligentsia feels constraint, a limitation of its horizons, such that its gaze turns inward and the issue becomes, not "what should I do and how can I affect the world?" but "how and why do I do what I do?" This was the situation, after 1945 but especially after 1968, of the French intelligentsia, whose ideas have been peculiarly influential in the United States. The French had lost an empire in Southeast Asia and North Africa, and the domain of the French language was marginalized by the scientific and commercial imperium of English. In French thought, poststructuralism succeeded structuralism, which had itself displaced Marxism, whose gods in the Soviet Union were to fail; each moment overlapped the next. With each step, the world receded. The intelligentsia came to tend its own garden, which it noticed was overgrown with words. Words became the world, which fed an old temptation and gift in French culture, one that Sartre remembered in his autobiography: "For a long time I mistook language for the world. To exist was to have a registered trade-name somewhere in the infinite Tables of the Word." Observation of the world meant not investigating it, which had been the first program of the *Annales* group, but "catching living things in the trap of phrases."[3] Poststructuralism has deep roots in French culture. Given the political importance of language in a country where, in 1789, most Frenchmen did not speak French exclusively, given the power of the traditional literary canon, but given also the respect for intellectuals in a centripetal culture, poststructuralism has its danger even in Paris but also cultural capital to use and work against.

The translation of ideas designed for France to the American situation was curious, because inapt. Here the intellectual has shallow cultural roots, here there is and has always been cultural decentralization, here words tend to the pragmatic. In the expansiveness of the 1960s, the American intellectual had some sense of making headway in the culture, morally and professionally, a sense that for feminists has lasted almost to this day. But now, like the French after 1945, the American intelligentsia inhabits a more paltry universe. The academy, for those within it, seems to blot out the world. The intellectual excitement of the moments when Marxism, black history, then feminism established a technique by which to expand intellectual horizons and redefine canons, that excitement is expiring. The once powerful and morally compelling cry, "here is a neglected group," which once spoke on the streets of Selma, now wanes in conviction, because it speaks in the alleyways of MLA committees. It has become the rallying cry of what is often the ward politics of professionalism. And this is not all to the bad, remembering that ward politics is the stuff of a working democracy, and that it is important to decide who gets the jobs, which group has the mayoralty, which kinship network or gender runs the jails and fills in the potholes. All this is important, but it is not the stuff of intellectual excitement. Now there is constraint. And now we have the linguistic turn, a way of exploring ourselves because our habitual way of exploring others has grown stale and predictable.

Southerners and those who study the South live in this wider world, too, and have been touched by it. Anne Jones's work, in particular, has been distinguished by an attempt to assimilate the wider currents of feminism and critical theory, but to make them work to render the South's literature and history intelligible. Others have been struggling with this issue.[4] But the present scholarship of Southern intellectual culture seems resistant to the more narcissistic dilemmas of recent methodology. About the purpose of scholarship, its justification and usefulness, these essays betray no anxiety. There seems to be little problem about methodological isolation. Most evidently, there is a belief that, above all, history and literary study are habitually relevant one to another, and so both historians and literary critics should converse, surrendering a little of their disciplinary identity in so doing. Historians write of fiction, as Joyner does; literary critics write of history, as Jones does.

So those who study Southern thought seem not fully to share the sense of constraint evident elsewhere. To the contrary, one sees energy being released. So little has been done, so much needs to be written about, both old-fashioned things and newfangled things. In such a situation fluidity seems to be necessary, fluidity between disciplines and subdisciplines, time and place, black and white, male and female. And fluidity, though sometimes alarming, is invigorating. Our authors are not dead, we have narratives, texts, readers, a society, contexts, meaning. Quite like old times.

And yet, the Webb lecturers do live in more than the logic of the subdiscipline of Southern intellectual history. There are these unresolvable anxieties that dwell in American society and Southern history, the sharp tensions of race and gender. (Class, as is usual with Americans, runs a poor and neglected third.) These essays, as I read them, seem to suggest an unstable solution to intractability; they seem to say that we can find a way to persist in the midst of failure and conflict, that we can call upon a personal and creative resilience when the public realm is disordered. The market economy darkens the world, but Johnson Jones Hooper finds a way to laugh. Louisa McCord finds herself subject to "an animal in pantaloons, every way her inferior," but writes a poem, a play, an article that holds herself together, tautly. William Alexander Percy converts the secret lacerations and pleasures of his homosexuality into the elusive elegances of *Lanterns on the Levee*. William Styron uses the "imbalances in his own life" to create "an act of willed empathy not only with Nat Turner but also with such writers as Ralph Ellison and Richard Wright."

This is an old problem, with an old solution. Consider David Hume, who as a young man retreated to the Scottish countryside to undertake the investigations that would eventuate in *A Treatise of Human Nature*. He shut himself away from society, concentrated his thoughts upon the nature of thought, upon metaphysics: he even, it has been suggested, experimented with his diet to gauge the effect of body upon mind. He found reason disintegrated at the touch. He wrote:

> Let our first belief be never so strong, it must infallibly perish by passing thro' so many new examinations, of which each diminishes somewhat of its force and vigour. When I reflect on the natural fallibility of my judgement, I have less confidence in my opinions, than when I only consider the objects concerning which I reason; and when I proceed still farther, to turn the scrutiny against every successive estimation I make of my faculties, all the rules of logic require a continual diminution, and at last a total extinction of belief and evidence.

Mind and man were "nothing but a bundle or collection of different perceptions, which succeed each other with an inconceivable rapidity, and are in perpetual flux and movement." But Hume also observed that the imagination necessarily intruded belief:

> Most fortunately it happens, that since reason is incapable of dispelling these clouds, nature herself suffices to that purpose, and cures me of this philosophical melancholy and delirium, either by relaxing this bent of mind, or by some avocation, and lively impression of my senses, which obliterate all these chimeras. I dine, I play a game of back-gammon, I converse, and am merry with my friends; and when after three or four hours' amusement, I wou'd return to these speculations, they appear so cold, and strain'd, and ridiculous, that I cannot find in my heart to enter into them any farther.

As in his philosophy, so in his life, Hume turned increasingly from metaphysics to society, from the *Treatise* to the *Essays Moral, Political, and Literary*, and eventually to the *History of England*.[5]

Survival and the making of things. They are not enough. But they are what we can have, if we try, and the world permits.

What's So Funny?

Southern Humorists and the Market Revolution

CHRISTOPHER MORRIS

"Stranger . . . did you ever see the *Yellow* Blossom from Jasper? . . . I'm the boy . . . perhaps a *leetle*, jist a *leetle*, of the best man at a horse-swap that ever trod shoe-leather. . . . Well, my old coon, do you want to swap *hosses?* . . . Well, fetch up your nag, my old cock; you're jist the lark I wanted to get hold of. I am perhaps a *leetle*, jist a *leetle*, of the best man at a horse-swap that ever stole *cracklins* out of his mammy's fat gourd. Where's your *hoss?*" The roaring Yellow Blossom addresses himself to an old man who examines Bullet, Blossom's handsome and feisty steed. The swap is on, and when it is over, it would appear that Blossom is right, that he is "jist a *leetle*, of the best man at a horse-swap." When the traders remove their saddles to switch them to their new mounts, a six-inch festering sore is revealed on the back of Blossom's horse Bullet. A crowd of spectators breaks into laughter at the old man's expense, encouraged by the irrepressible Yellow Blossom. The old man says nothing. But his son, who has quietly watched the whole affair, cannot contain himself any longer, and announces to the crowd: Bullet's back is "mighty bad off; but dod drot my soul if he's put it to daddy as bad as he thinks he has," for Kit, the horse the old man traded, is "both blind and *deef*, I'll be dod drot if he ein't!" And so the last laugh is on the Yellow Blossom.

"Stranger," says the old man, "don't mind what the little boy says. If you can only get Kit rid of them little failings you'll find him all sorts of a horse. You are a *leetle* the best man at a horse-swap that ever I got hold of."[1]

Augustus B. Longstreet of Georgia published "The Horse-Swap" in 1835. Nearly two decades later, another Southern writer, Joseph G. Baldwin, published his variation on the horse-trade story, titled "An Equitable Set-Off." Rather than a big-mouthed, bragging trader and his quiet victim, Baldwin presented two "enterprising" businessmen "in the horse-trading line," Mr. Smith and Mr. Hickerson. Smith, we are told as the story begins, has already had dealings with Hickerson and come up short. When he hears that Hickerson, "in the course of one of his trading forays in the neighboring village, had got a fine mule," Smith sees an opportunity for revenge. He enlists the aid of a confederate, who pretends to happen upon Hickerson and his new mule. "I see you have got Jones's big mule—Jones came near selling him to me, but I got item in time, and escaped." Hickerson asks him to explain and is told that "the mule does very well except in the full of the moon, and then he takes fits which last about a week, hardly ever longer; and then such rearing and charging, and biting and kicking! he's like all possessed—nobody and nothing can manage him." The man suggests he take the mule to Smith and trade him for the "bran-new sorrel horse he's got," which he does, and winds up giving away a perfectly good mule for a horse with "all the diseases that horseflesh is heir to, and some it gets by adoption." And so Mr. Smith has his revenge. But the story does not end there. When he learns what has happened, an angry Hickerson sues Smith in a court of law. The decision is for the plaintiff, however, on the grounds that Smith "had only obtained an equitable set-off" for an earlier deal.[2]

Nearly twenty years after Baldwin wrote his sketch, Mark Twain published yet another variation on the horse-trade tale, one based on personal experience. In a chapter in *Roughing It* he recalls how he was once "resolved to buy a horse." A sharp trader convinced him that what he really ought to have was a "Genuine Mexican Plug." "I did not know what a Genuine Mexican Plug was, but there was something about this man's way of saying it, that made me swear inwardly that I would own a Genuine Mexican Plug, or die." When he inquired into the advantages of such a horse, the trader replied: "He can out-buck anything in America!" It did not occur to Twain that perhaps bucking was not such an advantage. Needless to say, he ended up with the horse, but was unable to stay in the saddle. In just a few moments the rider bounced way up into the air only to return and find "the Genuine Mexican Plug was not there." The whole town witnessed Twain's ride, and his not-so-graceful dismount, and so when he realized he had been suckered by the horse trader, he could not find anyone willing to take the horse off his hands. To make matters worse, the Genuine Mexican Plug's appetite was as big as his buck. He started eating Twain into bankruptcy. Fortune finally appeared in the form of "a passing Arkansas emigrant," who, ignorant of the advantages of a Genuine Mexican Plug, took the horse off Twain's hands.[3]

In the first half of the nineteenth century the United States underwent a remarkable transformation, what historians have called "the market revolution." They mean by the term the development of a national market economy with all its consequences for American society and culture. The word revolution is appropriate; change was rapid, thorough, and to many who lived through it, utterly mystifying.[4] Nineteenth-century humorists helped readers confront the market and the social changes it entailed by showing them how to laugh at an otherwise very scary world. The stories of Southern humorists may be read on two levels. First, by identifying what was so funny, what were the targets of the humor, the butts of the jokes, we can see what the Americans of that period worried about. Second, by reading them as evidence of moral visions, or ideologies, we can learn from them how some antebellum Americans struggled to locate the capitalist market within their particular understanding of their world.

Each horse-trade story involves an exchange. Horse traders attracted special attention from writers because they were notorious; they were the used car dealers of their day. But the commodity exchanged is of no concern to us. What does matter is the representation of the exchange, which is quite different in each tale. In the first, the swap between Yellow Blossom and the old man is only secondarily an economic matter. Certainly, profit is not the point; sport is. We laugh because the young braggart is matched by an unassuming elderly man. But they might as well have arm wrestled. The second story is quite different. It involves two men who make a living trading horses. Making money is their business. Of course, the business becomes a game and egos are involved. Nevertheless, just when we might think this is all good fun, we are told of the lawsuit. Indeed, the seriousness of the traders becomes funny. The final story, by Mark Twain, is different still. It is the only one of the three to involve cash.

We are told how much Twain paid for the Genuine Mexican Plug—
$27. In addition, we learn that boarding the horse cost him $15 and
feeding the voracious beast cost $250. There was no contest in Twain's
story. Two men of even skill and wile did not face each other as in
the first two stories. Twain was clearly outmatched, and the trader
knew it. That was his business. Together, the stories present the development of the market and its effects on social relations.

The three stories also indicate an ideological shift. Longstreet's
story, which pits the loudmouthed Yellow Blossom against the quiet
gentleman, emphasizes social traits, not business acumen, because
character, not money, indicates quality. The second story places a
greater emphasis on business, so much so that neither trader seems
to possess any strength of character. Yet, neither are they villains.
Baldwin, it would appear, was less certain than was Longstreet of the
relationship between character and the market, though he was very
sure that the market was important. Twain reconnected morality and
the market, and in a way familiar to us. His story presents a modern
exchange. Anyone who has bought a car, especially if it turned out to
be a lemon, knows exactly how Twain felt. We laugh not only because
we understand that buyers should beware, but also because we fear
that we, like Twain, might get taken. Yet, though we may not always
like them, shady business people are accepted as part of our society.
Our defense is not to banish them from it, but to prepare ourselves
to deal with them. When we laugh at a saddle-sore Twain we are, in
part, laughing at ourselves.[5]

By 1850 or so the market revolution was most advanced in the
Northeast. It was no coincidence, then, that America's literary renaissance, which in many ways emerged as a reaction to it, occurred
in that region.[6] Yet, the market revolution inspired writers elsewhere, too. William Gilmore Simms, the antebellum South's most
prolific novelist, often debated the impact of money, commerce, and
materialism on society and on human character, especially in his border romances about frontier Georgia and Alabama.[7] But while romantic writers North and South waxed philosophical about the human
character and soul in an increasingly commercial world, and in so
doing tended to abstract their literature from the context of early
nineteenth-century American society, it was left to the humorists,
especially those from the South and Southwest, to present more real-
istic images of the market revolution.

Before the Civil War, humorists were most associated with the
frontier, especially in the South, where forests, Indian lands, and pio-

neer farms succumbed rapidly to commercial development in the form of cotton plantations. Perhaps the market revolution had its most disturbing impact in Southwestern frontier areas where it rapidly consumed the nonmarket, semisubsistent economy and society of pioneer communities. On the Southern frontier, in other words, the market revolution was particularly quick, jarring, and confusing. And if confusion can be frightening, it can also be very funny. In addition, because most readers lived in the East, the setting of so many humorist stories in what was then known as the Southwest—Alabama, Mississippi, Arkansas, and Louisiana—eased the trauma of the market revolution by making it seem more remote, less disconcerting, more humorous.[8]

So, what did Southern humorists make fun of? What was so funny? There are several recurring themes and images in this body of literature, which suggest the ways that Southerners perceived the market revolution and its effects on society. Humorists responded to the intrusion of the market economy into the world of Southern rural white men by lashing back at all who lived outside that world: slaves, Indians, city folk, Yankee peddlers, and especially women.

In early nineteenth-century America, market development proceeded with a general demand for consumer goods. In fiction, however, the desire for manufactured products is almost always feminine. In one story, for example, a yeoman farmer visits Augusta to sell a little cotton so he can make some purchases for his wife and daughters. "The Old lady wanted a pair of spectacles," the narrator tells us, "and the gals a bonnet each—ribbons and flowers, thread, buttons &c, *had* to be purchased" [emphasis added]. In another story the protagonist attends a camp meeting and makes off with the donations because his wife "informed him that 'the sugar and coffee was nigh about out,' and there were not 'a dozen j'ints and middlins, *all put together,* in the smoke-house.'" One humorist described a Tennessee mountain farm wife who "patterns arter all new fangl'd fashuns she hears tell on frum bussils tu britches." Even the wife and daughter of Mike Hooter forced the larger-than-life bear hunter to keep them in regular supply of petticoats and hair oil, although Mike, no average henpecked backwoodsman, avoided the market by providing bearskin lingerie and bear oil hair styler.[9]

Women, it seems, were to blame for pushing their men into the market economy, or so the stories go. In portraying women as consumers, Southern humor reflected in part the change in women's roles in a commercializing society, which in rural regions were in some ways more dramatic than were corresponding changes in men's roles. The market did displace much of the productive labor of farm women by transforming them, for example, from candle and cloth makers into candle and cloth buyers. And the labor women continued to do somehow seemed less visible, if no less real and arduous than that of men. Meanwhile, men continued in their capacity as producers—hunters, fishers, herders, farmers—even though more of the fruits of their labor went to market each year.[10]

The market did create a more clearly defined gender division of labor, and the humorist sketches certainly reflect that. But there was more to the representation of women in this literature. The transformation of farm wives from producers into consumers was easily exaggerated. Augustus B. Longstreet actually warned male readers against marrying the "Charming Creature," a woman who delighted in tea parties, balls, reading, playing the piano, taking trips to New York and Philadelphia, but who never worked. One such "Charming Creature," he wrote, drove her husband to bankruptcy and a drunkard's early death. However, most antebellum women never stopped producing even when they became responsible for buying household needs. The more cloth they bought, the more clothes they made. The more flour they purchased, the more cakes they baked. The more candles they brought home from the store, the more light they had by which they could work into the night preserving fruit in factory-made jars. Moreover, though minimized by Southern humorists, the desires of men for consumer goods were real and strong.[11]

As all farmers knew or soon discovered, participation in a market economy meant a loss of independence as they placed themselves and their families at the mercy of merchants, creditors, bankers, and fluctuating prices. Men risked, in other words, the basis of male authority within the home. They jeopardized their very manhood. By portraying women as the most aggressive consumers, humorists and their male readers surely projected their own desires for market goods as well as their fears of the emasculating power of the market on their wives and daughters so they could maintain an illusion of themselves as contented, independent men and semisubsistence producers with firm control over their households.

Male apprehension about participation in a market economy appeared in stories about the simple farmer clad in homespun who utterly rejected newfangled, that is to say, factory-made clothes. But if homespun could indicate proud rejection of the market, it could also represent lower-class poverty, ignorance, and, in effect, social impotence. The market was something to be feared; it was also to be mastered. Such ambivalence toward clothes, of course, extended to the women who were responsible for dressing their families. Thus, men whose hardworking wives provided their families with homemade clothes were hicks, but men who purchased garments for their families were driven to do so by lazy, if charming, and certainly nagging wives.[12]

Humorists also displaced fears of the market onto merchants, most of whom, in their stories, were Yankees. In one tale a yeoman farmer acquires the reputation of a sharp businessman when he bests a Yankee horse trader, only to lose it when he gambles away his year's earnings to a Yankee thimble player. A character in another story has nothing good to say about any "cussed, palaverin, inyun-eatin Yankee pedlar, all Jack-nife an' jaw . . . wif a carryall full ove appil-parin-mersheens, jewsharps, calliker, ribbons, sody-powder, an' uther durn'd truck." He acquires some of the peddler's soda powder, which he eats with water and then erupts in a froth like a human champagne bottle. "A Yankee pedlar's soul," he claims, "wud hev more room in a turnip-seed to fly roun in, than a leather-wing bat hes in a meetin-hous." In another story the same Yankee peddler-hater tells about a friend, a newlywed, who bought from a Yankee trader some "rare ripe Garden-Seed," which promised to make all his vegetables grow twice as fast. He discovered that the Yankee seeds even worked on people. When he returned from a trip of several weeks to find he had a baby daughter, he asked his wife to explain how this could have happened, given that they had been married just four and a half months. She explained to him the wonders of rare ripe garden seed. Peddlers brought all kinds of new products to once-isolated farmers. Though none would have been so mystified by them as were the characters of these stories, nevertheless, as the avant-garde of the market, peddlers represented another world, one semisubsistence farmers reached for but at the same time tried to keep at arm's length.[13]

Humorists also targeted city folk, as well as such marginal members of Southern male society as Indians and slaves. "Speaking of Mechanicsburg," says Mike Hooter in a story by William Hall, "the people down in that mud hole ain't to be beat no whar this side o' Christmas. I've hearn o' mean folks in my time, an' I've preached 'bout 'em a few; but, ever sense that feller Bonnel sold me a pint of red'eye whiskey—an' half ov it backer juice—fur a coonskin, an' then guv me a brass picayune for change, I've stoped talkin." In "The Thimble Game," by T. W. Lane, a Georgia farmer ventures into the jungles of Augusta and there loses his crop to a sharp gambler. Like Lane, Augustus Baldwin Longstreet was certain that cities offered no viable alternative to the violent backwoods.[14]

Indians were, in Johnson Hooper's stories about Simon Suggs, "the untutored children of the forest" cheated over and over again by wily white speculators. Yet, they were hardly innocent. Their desire for calico frocks, ribbons, and silver buckles, as well as "a waywardness, amounting to absolute stupidity," attracted hordes of shady characters, and thus the market, into the backcountry. Hooper had little use for them. Not surprisingly, he made Simon Suggs's first victim a slave, who, like the Indians, was incapable of fending for himself and was therefore to blame for his helplessness. Mark Twain also presented slaves as victims, though to be pitied rather than despised for their innocence in matters of money. If humorists could fault peddlers and speculators with bringing unwanted change, they could also accuse Indians, slaves, and women of naively inviting them into the Southern backcountry.[15]

Much more troubling to many early nineteenth-century Southern white men than the Yankee peddlers, materialistic women, or naive slaves and Indians was the paper money exchanged for market products and the credit system that enabled people to participate in the market apparently without any money whatsoever. Fear of banks and bank notes was well founded. The system of national finance was truly chaotic. Every bank issued its own notes, which, though used as money, were not in fact legal tender but only promises to pay legal tender, in the form of gold and silver specie, when presented to the bank that originally issued them. Shipping notes back to their bank of origin was risky and costly. The original bank might no longer be in business. For this reason no bank was required to take the notes of other banks. Thus, a national market developed without a national system of currency exchange. Rapid expansion of the economy, high inflation, frequent bank closings, mishandling of finances by honest businessmen, embezzlement by dishonest ones, shady land deals, and governments uncertain of their role in the economy, all undermined trust in paper currency, the institutions that printed it, and the people who traded it. Yet, one could not participate in the market economy and avoid this unstable banking and currency system.[16]

The cash-and-credit economy proved to be an endless source of humor for antebellum Southern storytellers. A Mississippi author made light of the complexity of the economy by imagining a conversation between a backwoods hunter and a bear. Says the hunter to his victim, "the ile what's in your hide would slick the har of all the galls in our neck of the woods 'til the cows come home. You carry a most too much dead capital in that ar skin of yourn, any how; and if it's the same to you, I'll just peel the bark off'n you, and larn you the rudiments of perlitical economy." A story by another Mississippi writer presented a conversation between a poor and ignorant Chunkey who cannot understand that paper money is bogus and the wise Governor who seeks to teach him the true value of hard specie. "Dam the specie currency," says Chunkey, "it aint no account, and I'm agin it. When we had good times I drank five-dollar-a-gallon brandy, and had pockets full of money." "But," says the Governor, "you bought the brandy on credit and never paid for it!" "What's the difference?" asks Chunkey! "Them what I bought it from never paid for it; they bought it on a credit from them foreigners, and never paid for it, and them foreigners, you say, are a pack of scoundrels, and I go in for ruinin' em, so far as good licker is concerned." Of course, Chunkey is much wiser than he seems, for he articulates what many Americans at the time believed to be the cause of the financial panic of 1837 and the depression that followed. The author was a former governor of Mississippi and member of the Democratic Party who, like so many supporters of that party, fought against the circulation of paper currency because he believed it led to the sort of irresponsible abuses represented by Chunkey and the "pack of scoundrels" who bought and sold on credit. In another story that poked fun at the monetary system and the general suspicion of it, the protagonist is hired by a newly opened bank to help put into circulation $2,000 worth of the institution's notes. He plans to do this by posing as a rich planter seeking to purchase slaves for his plantation, and then buy slaves with the bank notes, thereby establishing the currency's legitimacy. The sale is a sham. He purchases several slaves from a confederate. No one falls for the trick, however. Public suspicion that the notes are worthless remains. So he sells the slaves he purchased with worthless bills for sound currency and then vanishes, leaving the bankers who hired him with neither their money nor their slaves.[17]

No one understood the capitalist market economy as well as Simon Suggs, the creation of Alabama newspaper editor Johnson Jones Hooper. Humorists typically portrayed their heroes as innocently honest, or if self-serving, like Chunkey, so naive and incompetent as to be laughable. Simon Suggs, however, represents a very different character, an antihero. His motto, "it is good to be shifty in a new country," contrasts with the creed more often associated with Southern frontiersmen such as Davy Crockett—"Be always sure you're right—then go ahead!"

Simon Suggs excels at taking other people's money, and he preys on the insecurity and ignorance of others in a world in which few know what they are doing, including speculators and bankers, whom one might expect to be sharper. He lives in a world in which people are familiar with doing business face-to-face with associates they know, or at least know of. The national market economy depersonalizes business, destroying the face-to-face way of life; nevertheless, that is the way the people whom Suggs encounters want to live because that is how they continue to understand the world. Into the gap between old habits and a new reality steps Simon Suggs, the supreme confidence man, always passing for someone whom others desperately want to believe they know. (No one ever asks Suggs for two pieces of I.D., as he would be asked in our world.) Thus a banker in need of a favor gives Suggs a bribe because he is absolutely certain he can recognize a member of the state legislature when he sees one. And a young man hands over his money when he mistakes Suggs for his uncle General Thomas Witherspoon, the rich hog drover from Kentucky, while onlookers watch in envy, thinking how "desirable a thing it would be, to lend money to General Thomas Witherspoon, the rich hog drover." In his most famous assumed identity, Suggs becomes a convert at a camp meeting and makes off with the cash box (a scene recreated by Twain in *Adventures of Huckleberry Finn*).[18]

One story in particular portrays very clearly the confusion of the antebellum monetary system. "A Quarter Race in Kentucky," by Thomas Kirkman, was one of the most famous pieces of antebellum humor. The story first appeared in William T. Porter's magazine, *Spirit of the Times*, in 1836, the year the charter for the second Bank of the United States expired, leaving the country without a national bank system, hastening a financial collapse that ended the greatest burst of economic expansion to date, and ushering in a depression that lasted five years. Whether intended by the author or not—and the date of publication and politics of the author suggest it was—the story is a wonderful allegory for the craziness of the Jacksonian economy.[19] The Colonel tells of a time he attended a horse race between two riders, each of whom raised $300 in stakes. They were cheered on by a crowd of spectators who, in addition to putting up the stakes, made a lot of side bets among themselves. The Colonel joined the fun by offering $10 on the bay and was matched by Big Wash, who favored the sorrel. Big Wash offered to hold the bet, and the Colonel agreed. After the sorrel won a very close race, the losing rider announced he could not locate the men who put up his stake, and so he would not be able to pay the prize to the winner. Then the fun began. "Babel was a quiet retired place compared with the little assemblage at this time," we are told. "Some bets were given up, occasional symptoms of a fight appeared, a general examination was going on to be assured the knife was in the pocket, and those hard to open were opened and slipped up the sleeve; the crowd clustered together like a bee-swarm." But before matters got out of control, the officials who declared the winner changed their decision and declared a tie. All bets were off. This apparently pleased everyone, because the crowd cheered and adjourned to the bar.

The characters encountered by the Colonel in Kirkman's story all correspond to elements of society during the age of Andrew Jackson. The losing rider and those who bet on his horse were the debtors, many of whom could not make good on their payments because, like their losing rider, they could not locate the people who owed them or the banks that issued the notes. The original winners of the race represented the creditors. Both sides felt cheated and were prepared to fight for what they thought they were owed, until the judges, who stood for the Old Hero himself, Andrew Jackson, stepped in and almost magically changed the outcome of the race to everyone's satisfaction. Peace was restored. If only it had been as easy for Jackson when he killed the monster bank to place all debtors and creditors on an equal footing.

Thomas Kirkman's story appears to have been an attack on Andrew Jackson's decision not to renew the charter of the second Bank of the United States. That decision was, he seems to have suggested, silly and naive. It worked to solve problems of debt and rampant speculation only to the extent that the American people, like the spectators at the horse race who accepted the judges' final decision, wanted to believe that it worked. As the story relates, the Colonel and Big Wash were not fooled by the charade. While the crowd headed for the bar, Big Wash pocketed the Colonel's ten dollars to save it for the next day at the track. When the Colonel realized that Big Wash still had his money, Big Wash was nowhere to be found. The Colonel returned to the track the next day, and there placing bets on the races was Big Wash, who claimed, of course, to have lost the Colonel's money. When the Colonel suggested that perhaps Wash ought not to have bet money that did not belong to him, Wash pulled a giant Bowie knife from his belt, began whittling a stick of cedar, and said that he hoped the Colonel was not challenging his integrity. The Colonel, his eye on Big Wash's knife, said he was not and agreed to accept Wash's I.O.U. in good faith. But like the horse race, this settlement was a sham. Wash's promissory note was worthless, as both men knew. No one would accept it as tender. But Wash pretended, because so many still believed, that personal attributes still had value in an exchange. But reputation, honor, integrity, all valuable attributes in a traditional pre-market economy that was essentially local in scope, so that reputations could be known by all traders, were of little value in a national market economy. Big Wash understood the ways of the new market society, but could speak in traditional language, and was perfectly willing to do so if he could profit by it. Thus he emerged as the only winner in a race in which the judges declared and everyone believed there were no winners or losers. Wash represented the shady businessman who, in Kirkman's view, profited from the financial instability caused by the naïveté of Andrew Jackson and his supporters. The Colonel, who represented the Whig opposition to the party of Jackson, realized that without a centrally directed financial system there was no way to protect people such as himself from profiteers such as Wash. "I wish you would try Wall Street with this paper," he mutters sarcastically to the reader at the story's close. "I wish to cash it; but I'll run a mile before I wait for a quarter race again."

Altogether, these stories indicate what antebellum Southerners found so upsetting about the rapid development of a capitalist market economy—its instability and unpredictability, the shady characters it spawned, the suspicion that it forced people to take into their encounters with other people. The stories suggest how Americans explained these upsetting changes. They were the fault of materialistic, superficial women, ignorant Indians and slaves, slick Yankee peddlers, and foreign merchants. The stories also explain how the market, which imposed itself on peoples' lives, imposed itself on their ways of thinking. The market economy challenged and altered the moral universe of nineteenth-century Americans.

As humorists, Longstreet and Kirkman had much in common. They both wrote with a moral vision fashioned before the nation's transition to a national capitalist market economy was completed, though they could see that transition happening. Both were somewhat detached from the societies they described in their fiction. Both told their stories from the perspective of what historian Kenneth Lynn has called the "Self-controlled Gentleman," the narrator and/or hero who manages to rise above the crazy and funny situations he encounters, and then make sense of it all for the reader. Both critiqued the emerging capitalist market economy and the liberal democratic society to which it gave birth, preferring instead the hierarchical republican order of the eighteenth century, vestiges of which persisted in the older plantation regions of the South in which they lived. Nevertheless, their similar styles and themes notwithstanding, the substance of their critiques and the solutions they offered are quite different.[20]

Thomas Kirkman's character, Big Wash, enjoyed playing the ponies, but what he really had fun doing was playing with money. Thus he was a far different creature than the big-mouthed Yellow Blossom who traded horses for sport in Augustus Baldwin Longstreet's story. They belonged to different eras, and perhaps to different economies. Yellow Blossom traded horses in a world in which exchange was as much if not more a social than economic matter. He did not trade for profit or for a living but for his sense of himself as a swaggering, independent man. Big Wash only pretended to be concerned about self-image so he could keep the Colonel's ten dollars. The two characters, and so their creators, inhabited different moral universes, reflecting the transformations wrought by the market revolution.

Writing in the early 1830s about society in and around Augusta, Georgia, twenty years earlier, Longstreet looked back on those violent, boisterous days with some regret at lost innocence, but mostly with confidence that newly settled regions did eventually become civilized, by which he meant controlled, ordered, genteel. Like the heroes of William Gilmore Simms's romantic novels, Longstreet's "Self-controlled Gentleman" is a man of the eighteenth century, an admirer of the society dominated by colonial gentlemen. The backcountry regions he visits and describes are more like those of early national, not Jacksonian America. Thus, Longstreet looked back not just to middle Georgia in the early nineteenth century, but beyond that to the hierarchical, orderly world of the eighteenth-century gentleman. Money and the market have little to do with life in the world storied by Longstreet because they just did not seem as important as manners and character. His tales only hint at the market revolution to come and seem to suggest that it will bring moral chaos, not just to the backcountry but to settled regions as well. Though generally critical of frontier society for its lack of social order, Longstreet described a country dance given by a local magistrate and his family at their single-room cabin much more favorably than he described a city ball. In the country, "all were invited to dance." "Occasionally some sharp cuts passed between the boys, such as would have produced half a dozen duels at a city ball; but here they were taken as they were meant, in good humor." The midday dinner consisted of "plain fare, but there was a profusion of it," and around the table "old and young of both sexes seated themselves at the same time." The social order was perhaps too fluid for Longstreet's taste, but the company was certainly pleasant.[21]

A story about a ball in the city of Augusta presented a very different scene. Although the country dance was a haphazard, spontaneous affair, the city ball was completely orchestrated. Dance partners were prearranged, as was the time of appearance for each guest. The musicians were black, the dancers white. Time of arrival, the impression made upon entering the ballroom, one's dance partner, and personal appearance all indicated one's place in society. Yet this was not the social order Longstreet had in mind as cure for a disorderly backcountry. The competition to display superficial attributes of character was intense. One lady's late answer to a call by the dance manager precipitated an argument between two men that resulted in a duel. Backcountry roarers, drinkers, and fighters could be violent and crude, but they were often generous, and always genuine. The characters he identified in the city were utterly superficial and unworthy, indeed, incapable of bringing order to their society. That Longstreet found urban life to be artificial is at least an implicit criticism of the market and consumer society.[22]

Thomas Kirkman, unlike Longstreet, wrote not about the past but about the present. Nevertheless, Kirkman, like Longstreet, desired order, financial order, especially, from which social stability followed. Both shared a sense of moral confidence acquired before the development of a capitalist market and even employed the same narrative technique; yet, they were clearly writing about two very different times. Longstreet's early national aristocratic "Self-controlled Gentleman" would have been no more at home at Kirkman's horse race than he was in the Georgia backcountry. For Longstreet, morality had little to do with money, which in any case was scarce in early frontier Georgia. Kirkman wrote about the 1830s, a period of tremendous economic expansion, so for him morality had everything to do with money and whether one dealt in the promissory notes of strangers or in U.S. bank notes.

The financial and moral order that Kirkman desired would, he hoped, come from Henry Clay, the Whig Party, and the national market system that they and the elites who understood the interests of the nation sought to create.[23] Kirkman, therefore, wrote about the future. Indeed, many Southern humorists were members of the Whig Party that opposed the policies of Andrew Jackson. But their stories were much more than partisan appeals. Some writers in this vein actually belonged to the Democratic Party. Nevertheless, all described a nation in the throes of a market revolution that completely undermined the old order, and then they offered a solution. Intelligent, selfless men of character, not unlike the "Self-controlled Gentleman" of Longstreet's stories, would lead the way, not backward to a time when money did not matter, however, but forward to a new age when money and investment could be counted on as a measure of character because it would be controlled by men of character. Such writers, in short, found a place for the late eighteenth-century republican gentleman in the commercial world of the nineteenth century.

The moral confidence of the republican gentleman writers is missing in the stories by Johnson Jones Hooper and Joseph Glover Baldwin. The capitalist market did not approach Hooper and Baldwin; it already enveloped them. Longstreet believed traditional civilization would be restored, and Kirkman believed it could at least be adapted to a new market society; Hooper and Baldwin presented a completely new world in which traditional values made no sense. Yet they did not criticize that new society so much as they made fun of those who pretended it did not exist by continuing to live by outmoded ways and means. And they poked fun at those who were incompetent at fending for themselves in the new society. They implied that a new age had arrived and that, if it was to be managed at all, it would be done by new sorts of people operating by new standards. Exactly who those people and what those standards would be was uncertain. Hooper's character, Simon Suggs, is essentially amoral, guided only by his maxim, "it is good to be shifty in a new country." By "new country" he means not simply the new settlements in Alabama, but quite literally a brand-new country in which rules of behavior from earlier times and the old country to the east do not apply.[24] In *Flush Times* Baldwin portrays the Virginia gentlemen, the same sort of characters who are in such transcendent control in the stories by Longstreet, as utterly lost in frontier Alabama and Mississippi. Moreover, Hooper and Baldwin offered no hope that gentlemanly order would be restored. Kirkman's Colonel may have lost ten dollars to the unscrupulous Big Wash, but the reader is left with the sense that the loss was temporary. Hope remained so long as there were men of honor with good fiscal sense. In Hooper's stories there are no gentlemen because there are no standards of gentility. The world is divided into swindlers and marks, without regard to class, and when it comes to swindling, Simon Suggs, the preacher's son, is unmatched. That his escapades are presented in the form of a political biography, like those typically published in antebellum America by the friends of honorable though modest office seekers, mocks the pretentious claims of all gentlemen in the "new country."[25]

Moral confidence reappeared in the stories of Mark Twain, and, less overtly but in a similar way, in the stories about Sut Lovingood, written by George Washington Harris. But it was a very different morality from that of the earlier Southern story tellers. Sut Lovingood's world seems so foreign, even absurd, as almost to belong to another planet. The characters have no comprehension of profit, of making money. Sut's daddy, for example, is so lazy that when his horse dies he is thrilled, for now he cannot work. Eventually, though, he must plant if only to have something to eat, so he hitches himself to the plough and "acts horse."[26] The satire of Twain's novel, *The Gilded Age,* is directed at a political system that put incompetent people into positions of power; the book does not question the market economy.[27] Writing after the capitalist transformation of America was all but complete, Twain could critique the market economy and society from within it, secure in the notion that it was at heart morally sound and secure. The Duke and the King in *Huckleberry Finn,* the players of "The Royal Nonesuch," are hardly the dangerous if amusing nihilists that Simon Suggs is. They are themselves victims, harmless innocents who do not know as the reader does that they are about to be destroyed by a commercializing and industrializing America in which they no longer have a place. They are amusing not because they contradict society's values; the Duke and the King embrace them in their own way. But by the time of the robber barons, when Twain wrote, such characters were small time operators, amusing because they were so harmless.[28]

What we see in the literature of the Southern humorists is America's transformation into a capitalist market society. Much of Twain's humor is nostalgic, or so it has seemed to modern readers. The world Longstreet disdained, and Hooper feared, becomes in Twain's humor the playful "world we have lost" but one that we hope Huck will find because we cannot. Longstreet certainly never lit out for any territory to escape civilization. He would have identified less with Huck than with the widow Douglas, who struggled to bring order to the wilds of early Missouri and to a young boy. Hooper and Baldwin went west, but not for the reasons Huck did, not to find the past, or preserve the present, but to seek opportunity, to make money, just as did Twain when he ventured to Nevada and California. Longstreet would not have understood. Twain, of course, eventually moved East, to New York and Connecticut, a clear indication that he fully embraced a modern, capitalist America. Perhaps Hooper and Baldwin would have understood. Perhaps not.

In 1931 William Faulkner published a story about a horse trade. In "Spotted Horses" Flem Snopes returns to Frenchman's Bend with a stranger from Texas and a dozen or so wild ponies, "genuine Texas cockle-burrs," "wild as deer, deadly as rattlesnakes." The horses are clearly too much for Mississippi farmers more familiar with mules, though a crowd of men cannot resist bidding for them. When they learn that some of the women do not approve, the men in this story, as in so many of the nineteenth-century humorist sketches, assert their authority as if to blame women for their problems. In one scene a buyer alternately strikes with a coil of rope his new horse and his wife. And the men do have problems. They have lost control over their lives. By possessing such apparently uncontrollable horses they seek to reassert command over their beasts, over their women, and over their world. They hope to reclaim a sense of manhood that once was theirs, they believe, in an earlier time when Mississippi was a part of that West from which emerged the horses and the Texan with the pearl-handled pistol. These men are beaten, and though they do not realize it, the market is victorious. Some of them are desperately poor. "We got chaps in the house that never had shoes last winter," the wife of one buyer pleads to the Texan. "We aint got corn to feed the stock. We got five dollars I earned weaving by firelight after dark." The horses bring disaster. They escape from their pen and rampage for several days through the surrounding countryside. In one especially humorous scene a horse runs through Mrs. Littlejohn's boardinghouse. "Maybe there wasn't but one of them things in Mrs. Littlejohn's house that night," remarks Ratliff, one of the boarders. "But it was the biggest drove of just one horse I ever seen. It was in my room and it was on the front porch and I could hear Mrs. Littlejohn hitting it over the head with that washboard in the backyard all at the same time." Retorts another boarder, "Jumping out windows and running indoors in his shirttail? I wonder how many Ratliffs that horse thought he saw." "I dont know," says Ratliff. "But if he saw just half as many of me as I saw of him, he was sholy surrounded."[29]

The humor in this story, however, cannot mask a tragic tale of people struggling to survive. As the horses continue to run wild, one man lies near death, another is nearly run off a bridge but escapes with only a broken leg, while still another actually manages to catch his horse, by tripping it and breaking its neck. In the end, it is not the wild West of memory that beats the men and women of Frenchman's Bend, but Flem Snopes, the capitalist economy personified: "Flem would trim Eck or any other of his kin quick as he would us." Of course, everyone suspected as much all along, though they wanted to believe otherwise. They had banished him once, but he had returned and beaten them again. "I reckon there aint nothing under the sun or in Frenchman's Bend neither that can keep you folks from giving Flem Snopes and that Texas man your money," remarks Ratliff. He is right. The market could neither be resisted nor controlled. And that was not so very funny, after all.[30]

A "Dangerous Inmate" of the South:

Louisa McCord on Gender and Slavery

SUSAN A. EACKER

To the student of Southern history familiar with antebellum South Carolina's preeminent female intellectual, Louisa Susanna McCord, it might seem absurd to suggest that she could have anything in common with her contemporaries in the fledgling women's rights movement to the North, or for that matter with her own native state's fugitive sisters, Angelina and Sarah Grimké. The Grimké sisters, after all, would come to be resurrected by historians of women as the first female abolitionists and feminists in United States history to argue their causes in public before "promiscuous" or mixed sex audiences, while McCord's pen was more often brandished in published invectives against the doubly damning doctrines of abolition and women's rights than on any other subject.[1] Yet, more than a cursory reading of Louise McCord may reveal surprising similarities, both in life histories and ideological propensities, among these three women.

To begin with, both McCord and the Grimké sisters were born into prominent slaveholding families of Charleston, South Carolina, around the turn of the nineteenth century. The three also had strong, politically influential fathers who in turn greatly influenced their daughters' intellectual abilities and interests. Langdon Cheves, Louisa McCord's father, was president of the Bank of the United States under James Monroe. John Faucheraud Grimké was a successful Charlestonian lawyer and one-time South Carolinian legislator, and his son Thomas followed his father's vocation as a lawyer in the Cheves's law firm. And finally, all three most certainly flirted in the same social, political, and intellectual circles of antebellum Charleston, no doubt even playing the role of belle at the same Southern cotillions during their coming-out years. And yet they also shared something much more profound than Charleston, camellias, and coquetry, for in their writings on the subject of slavery was inextricably bound up the question of gender and the respective positions of male and female.

Few scholars of the antebellum South, and of the peculiar institution in particular, have paid adequate attention to the gendered dimensions of proslavery thought.[2] Yet in the words of historian Stephanie McCurry, "the subordination of women bore a great deal of the ideological weight of slavery."[3] That the subsumed status of women in the private sphere of the plantation household could bear any relationship to the public world of Southern slavery politics may appear problematic to those who still hold to a rigid distinction between the personal and the political, the private and the public. Yet as historian Joan W. Scott has noted, "The public-private distinction—families as compared to the nation, mother's needs versus the needs of the state . . . is critical in the formulation of nationalist or patriotic ideologies. To what extent these ideologies also rest on and reinscribe existing notions of gender relationships and the sexual division of labor remains an important—and as yet unstudied—question."[4]

In the attempt of the Old South's ideologues to bring into being just such a regionally conscious weltanschauung (and in the North's attempts to extinguish such an ideology), it was precisely the politics of the so-called private, gendered, and racial that so fiercely animated public debate both within and between both sides of the Mason-Dixon line. As a consequence, in the South, the circumscribed borders of conventional gender relations were as fiercely patrolled as the plantation's slave quarters; while in the North, in spite of an emerging discourse on the contested status of middle class women, none but the most radical Garrisonian abolitionists were prepared to make common cause with a nascent woman's rights movement. Not surprisingly, then, it was not just the proslavery argument of Southern ideologues that tended to coalesce around the axis of gendered difference, but the rhetoric of the North's abolitionist-feminists as well, at least in analogy if not intent. This is, it turns out, no less the case with Louisa McCord and Angelina and Sarah Grimké. Yet while Sarah Grimké could "rejoice, because I am persuaded that the rights of woman, like the rights of slaves, need only to be examined to be understood and asserted,"[5] for McCord, the nexus linking sex and race would lead to her warning that "the poison [the doctrine of women's rights] is spreading . . . and, it is but a piece with Negro emancipation. . . ."[6] Louisa McCord then, like other apologists for slavery, was well aware of, and in large measure responding to, the thoughts and writings of her Northern antagonists. It may be instructive, therefore, to situate McCord in counterpoint to the Grimkés, for while the line separating McCord from her transplanted Southern sisters may have demarcated two disparate cultures, the Mason-Dixon divide was not an impenetrable one, as ideas did flow in both directions.

Louisa McCord wrote and published on such topics as political economy, free trade, secession, slavery, and the anthropology of race, managing almost invariably to smuggle the "woman question" into her essays. While most historical treatments of McCord are concerned with the textual analysis of these political works (she wrote for such popular mid-nineteenth century Southern journals as the *Southern Quarterly Review, Southern Literary Messenger,* and *De Bow's Review)* it is only by foregrounding the more self-reflective McCord that emerges in her letters, poetry, and drama that we can fully illuminate the thought contained in her polemical pieces. Elizabeth Fox-Genovese, who has written of both the public and private McCord in *Within the Plantation Household,* concludes that McCord like other "handmaidens of the system" of Southern plantation paternalism, ultimately threw her lot in with her class and race rather than her sex. Admittedly, McCord may have identified with and thus mimicked the rhetorical style of her male proslavery peers by, in Fox-Genovese's words, writing "in the idiom of the canon."[7] Certainly a review of her expressly political writings, uninformed by her more private deliberations, would lead one to such a conclusion. But as a woman who hoped to be published and read in the South, such literary conformity was all but a necessity.[8] To read McCord solely on this level, then, is to miss many of the nuances in her work, which far from being transparent, contains multiple layers of meaning. Like nineteenth-century women novelists, McCord's position was one of conflicted authorship—engendered by an acute awareness of the paradoxical role which female publication necessarily demanded when private women stepped onto the public stage of the literati.[9] As feminist literary critics of the female genre of domestic fiction have shown, resolution of this conflict was typically played out in the work itself and took several forms: authorial anonymity through the use of pseudonyms (McCord used her initials L. S. M.) as well as the utilization of a formulaic plot of feminine conventionality that glossed over an undercurrent of discontent and subterfuge.[10] McCord, then, was as much aware as these female fiction writers that she was, to use Anne Goodwyn Jones's playfully sardonic metaphor, "dancing to someone else's music."[11] And in McCord's case, the composers were all Southern defenders of slavery.

For proslavery proponents in the blackbelt South, there seemed to be no dearth of historical material to draw upon in their rationalization for nineteenth-century slavery, which was buttressed, they claimed, by the transhistorical existence of human inequalities. Contemporary historians can, like the proslavery apostles of the South, find the gendered language of slavery manifested in a multitude of forms. For all over the South, beginning in the early nineteenth century, slavery's intellectual apologists began to move from a reactionary defense of human servitude as a "necessary evil" to an offensive (in both senses of the word) strategy whereby chattel slavery was somehow transformed into a "positive good."[12] In its clever linguistic repackaging, formal inequalities afforded the underlings of society (a category that in Virginian George Fitzhugh's words included, among others, "wives . . . lunatics . . . and . . . domestic slaves") a paternalistic and private form of protection that the law did not necessarily allow.[13] This kinder and gentler fictive version of the master-slave relationship was grounded in both Aristotelian philosophy and biblical scripture, and its promulgators, clergy and laity alike, including such prominent South Carolinians as James Henley Thornwell, James Henry Hammond, and William Harper, found no lack of justification in either body of works.[14] After all, the pious patricians of the Old Testament allowed for and even kept slaves themselves while Aristotle's conception of the household (that original building block of the state writ small), included "master and slave, husband and wife, father and children," who "from the hour of their birth" were either "marked out for subjection" or "for rule."[15] Proslavery theorists such as Fitzhugh, for example, found in Aristotle all the ideas that he thought "original with men" and thus argued that "two-thirds of mankind, the women and the children, are everywhere the subjects of family government. In all countries where slavery exists, the slaves are the subjects of this kind of government. Now slaves, wives and children have no other government; they do not come directly in contact with the institutions and rules of the State. But the family government, from its nature, has ever been despotic."[16]

In attempting to ameliorate these "despotic" tendencies of the male-dominated private sphere, particularly as it was instanced in the plantation household, domestic servitude, in its innumerable forms, was transformed into a kind of protection racket, as proslavery writers such as William Harper claimed that "the care of man gives the boon of existence to myriads who would never otherwise have enjoyed it."[17] Those "myriads"—slaves, the infirmed, and women—had actually struck a bargain made in a Southern heaven, for in giving up certain rights that their natural inferiorities prevented them from fully actualizing, they were assured benevolent treatment by the paterfamilias of the plantation, where the bonds of familiarity and affection resulted in a weighted sense of responsibility for his dependents, a responsibility which went beyond the mere strictures of formal legal obligation. Thus Harper, confident of the quiescence of the oppressed, could ask: "What is the foundation of the bold dogma [that inequality is a natural phenomena] so confidently announced? Females are human and rational beings. They may be found of better facilities, and better qualified to exercise political privileges, and to attain the distinctions of society, than many men; yet who complains of the order by which they are excluded from them?"[18]

The existence of a proslavery ethos grounded in antiegalitarian impulses within the family, particularly in women's subordinate status, seems indisputable, yet historians of the Old South disagree as to the actual appeal, dissemination, and material basis for such an analysis, based as it was on natural inequalities rather than racial ordering.[19] If, as influential writer Thomas Dew maintained in 1832, the introduction of black chattel slavery saved the inferior sex from a similar fate by merely replacing "the labor of the slave . . . for that of the woman" then how could the "mud-sill" stratum of southern society, or women of all classes for that matter, accept such a volatile doctrine that but for fortune might also enslave them?[20] Or was there not some common ground transcending the terrain of the plantation upon which male planters and yeoman alike could stand, thus assuring to each their own sphere of subordination?

Historian Gerda Lerner locates the transhistorical acceptance of slavery (first instanced in the slavery of women who were captured in war) by nonslaveholding males, who were themselves "dominated and exploited in regard to resources by more powerful men of their own group," in the former group's opportunity to "dominate and control. . . . the women and children of their own class."[21] Transplanting this argument from the archaic to the antebellum slave state, Stephanie McCurry maintains that slavery's appeal to the yeoman class of South Carolina (and one must assume the rest of the Old South as well) was assured not so much by the illusive hope that yeoman males might acquire dominion over their own Big House but by the recognition that they already held such sway, no matter how modest their dwelling, by masculine prerogative over their own dependent women and children. Thus whether they owned slaves or not, Southern men could find some solace in being the lords of their own households. As historian Catherine Clinton succinctly sums up the matter, "Cotton was King, white men ruled, and both white women and slaves served the same master."[22]

Traditionally, the coupling of women and slavery has been viewed by historians of the Old South as nothing more than a rhetorical analogy. Indeed, after the Grimké sisters claimed that women were but "the white slaves of the North," such analogies became familiar fare among later abolitionists and women's rights advocates and have even spilled over into the rhetoric and analysis of some twentieth-century feminists.[23] Although the *literal* comparison of women and slaves may be flawed, it was certainly more than just metaphoric coincidence that led some antebellum women in both the North and South to offer comparisons between racial and sexual subordination. Proslavery advocates, after all, surely used the analogy to strike a responsive chord with some Southerners. We thus need to ask to what extent the proslavery language of sexual difference corresponded to reality. For example, how did real women, and not just "woman" as textual representation, internalize and react to this language of subordination? For notwithstanding William Harper's confidence in the Southern system of gender compliance, there were still some white Southern women who would "complain of the order by which they are excluded."

It seems certain that even before Louisa McCord was old enough to understand or even analyze her discontent, she felt personally constrained by the limits placed upon her sex. All of the brief biographies on McCord mention the fact that at an early age she was found crouched behind a door, eavesdropping on her brothers' math lessons, and that her father finally determined that Louisa should be provided with comparable educational opportunities.[24] In the tightly circumscribed world of polite Southern society, the young Louisa chafed under the only acceptable role (and most certainly the restrictive adornment] for her gender—that of the belle. In a letter to her brother, written when she was still single at the relatively advanced age of twenty-nine, she expresses relief at temporarily being "released from playing belle, which . . . seems some how *[sic]* or other to be my destiny when I go into company."[25] McCord obviously preferred to mingle in the intellectual and political circles of her father and his peers—the Clays and Calhouns—or to spend her time overseeing Lang Syne, the plantation near Columbia left to her by an aunt. At the time Angelina Grimké's "Appeal to the Christian Women of the South" appeared in print in 1836, Louisa was playing the role of plantation mistress. There is no evidence that Louisa McCord read this epistle (it was banned and publicly burned in Charleston, and its author, now relocated to Philadelphia, forbidden to set foot again in her native city); nevertheless, it was expressly written for women slaveholders like McCord, "in order to arouse *you*, as the wives and mothers, the daughters and sisters, of the South, to a sense of your duty as *women* . . . on that great subject. . . ."[26]

It was no coincidence that Angelina's call resonated with many northern women, coming as it did in a time period when the new market economy was forcing men out of the private space of the household while at the same time sealing women's fate inside it. This polarization of the two spheres—the public one of the market and the private one of domesticity—served to delineate the proper gender roles of male and female, respectively, and although it lessened women's contributions to the economy and thus their comparative worth, it also tended to cede domestic authority and matters of the heart to the good wife and mother who was thus ideologically primed to respond to that greatest of moral causes—abolition. It was here at the hearth and home, thought Grimké, that the hearts of fathers, husbands, and brothers might "bend under moral suasion" and where women of the South "can overthrow this horrible system of oppression and cruelty, licentiousness and wrong" by "prick[ing] the slaveholders' conscience."[27]

If Louisa McCord's conscience as a slaveholder was ever pricked, she hid it well. From all available accounts she was an adept, even relatively humane, manager of her black dependents, giving out to each slave a weekly allowance of provisions, measuring feet for shoes, superintending the spinning and the weaving, the sick house, the children's day nursery, the blacksmith's and carpenter's shops, and, after her own three children were born, their education as well.[28] As her daughter would later write, "she kept the whole machinery going so smoothly."[29] That she was not quite content with plantation do-mesticity, however, comes across especially in McCord's private cor-respondence, unfiltered by the masculine lens of publication and the aura of anonymity demanded in her public works. In her assigned gender role as educational guardian, for example, she writes in a letter to a friend in 1852 of being "considerably bothered with the young ones": "I school them all the morning and of course in the afternoon am too *stupid* [emphasis mine] and tired to do anything for myself. So I am just school mistress until some other régime is established. Mr. McCord offers to read a little history and geography with them, but I do not count much upon his help. He does not like trouble much. . . ."[30]

Besides her private manifestations of discontent, McCord's public utterances can also be interpreted as subtle acts of insurrection. Be-fore she was married in 1840, Louisa expressed her talents and her grievances through poetry, and the only existing evidence of her literary skills for this time is a collection of poems later published in 1848 as *My Dreams*. These poems can be read as a deliberate working out and a somewhat resigned acceptance of the position to which her sex had consigned her, as can be seen in portions of "The Firefly" who, "not content with its lowly station," must nevertheless learn "how to check Ambition's flight" and "seek'st thus no forbidden height." Interpreted as a woman still railing against the gender segregation of Southern life, the final two verses of "The Firefly" de-serve full elaboration, if more for psychological insight than artistic merit:

> What though thou, like me, must find—
> Born to Earth, doomed to regretting—
> Vainly that the restless mind
> Seeks to soar, its birth forgetting.
>
> Visions bright to Earth exiled,
> Of fantastic hopes repented,
> *Let us to home be reconciled*
> *Learn at least to be contented.* [emphasis mine].[31]

That the "restless mind" of the firefly, seeking to forget its birth, was indeed McCord's own is confirmed in an 1848 letter to her friend William Porcher Miles, the same year that her poetry was published. Here she speaks of being "pushed back in every possibly way" and "endeavor[ing] for many a long year to crush my own propensit-ies. . . ." "An effortless life, is," she continues, "to a *restless mind* [em-phasis mine] a weary fate to be doomed to; and as no other door is open to me, I may as well push on at this."[32]

Up North the Grimké sisters found the portals to the public world closed to women as well. Believing that it was the "sex ques-tion" that was the primary obstacle in blocking the effective dissemi-nation of their antislavery message, thus keeping women from toiling in the vineyard for the slave, both sisters initially argued for the rights of women merely as an instrumental step necessary in overthrowing the bondage of their black brothers and sisters. This point becomes particularly evident in Angelina's private correspondence, as can be seen in her reply to Theodore Weld and John Greenleaf Whittier, who are apparently "greatly alarmed at the idea of our advocating the *rights of woman*." Angelina countered these male objections by in-sisting that "*We* cannot push abolitionism forward with all our might *until* we take up the stumbling block out of the road. . . . what *then* can *woman* do for the slave, when she is herself under the feet of man and shamed into *silence?*"[33] And in her "Appeal to the Women of the Nominally Free States," she would assert that "the denial of our duty to act, is a bold denial of our right to act and if we have no right to act, then may *we* well be termed 'the white slaves of the North'—for like our brethren in bonds, we must seal our lips in silence and de-spair."[34] Finally, in a series of letters to Catherine Beecher (written in rebuttal of Beecher's recently published work exhorting women to spend their time and talents in the proper management of their households), Angelina would proclaim her now famous axiom that the "investigation of the rights of the slave has led me to a better understanding of my own."[35]

The Grimké sisters' meteoric rise to antislavery stardom was comparatively short-lived, no doubt from fears for their personal safety. Angelina's last public speech on behalf of abolition came in May, 1838, the same month and year (perhaps not coincidentally) that she married Theodore Dwight Weld. Speaking for over an hour at the newly built Pennsylvania Hall in Philadelphia, Angelina's voice was constantly drowned out by an angry mob that pelted the windows with rocks and subsequently burned the building to the ground. After this, both sisters retired with Weld to a New Jersey farm and spent their lives in semiobscurity, although both continued to lend their support to the causes of abolitionism and women's rights. Sarah continued to write, particularly on the latter subject. Writing to a friend, Angelina rationalized her retreat into domesticity as a living testament to the fact that their dangerous foray into the exclusive male sphere of public politics had not "ruined" the sisters for the female private sphere.[36]

Whether it was Angelina's frightful experience with the politics of mob violence that night in Philadelphia that compelled the sisters to stop their public agitations, or the resistance both women encountered within their own ranks, it was exactly this type of outcome that Louisa Susanna McCord would ultimately warn about in her published injunctions against women's clamor for equality. In fact, in the only published reference to the Grimkés in all of McCord's works, she might well have been speaking directly to Angelina as she imagines a "gentle . . . Angelina, or Lucretia fairly pitted, in the Senate, against Mr. Foote, for instance, or Mr. Benton, or the valorous Houston, or any other mere patriot, whom luck and electioneering have foisted there. We do not doubt their feminine power, in the war of words . . . but are the ladies ready for a boxing match?"[37] That it was the ultimate male trump card of sheer physical superiority that made any notion of women's equal rights (in this case, their participation in the exclusively male arena of politics) a mere chimera was a constant theme played out in almost all of McCord's writings.[38] Whether from personal experience with corporeal male force (her husband was on occasion known to resort to fisticuffs with other men) or her gendered handicap even when it came to exerting her intellectual powers, McCord was as much aware as the Grimké sisters of the decided advantage of men in subduing the weaker sex, which, she admitted, had been "frequently, habitually . . . even invariably, oppressed and misused" by the male "in the unjust use of his strength."[39] Like her earlier poetic musings, much of her prose dealing with women seems to have been written to convince her audience of arguments she herself had personally formulated and accepted as a rationalization for the fact that, despite her capabilities or ambition, she could never hope to gain ascendancy in the male world of southern politics that constituted so much of her intellectual discourse.[40]

Bolstered by the insights gleaned from her private utterances, McCord's political writings, like her earlier poetry, can thus be read as an attempt to resolve this gendered predicament, as seen in her essay "Carey On the Slave Trade." The following passage of that essay encompasses and condenses almost her entire argument on both women and slavery, as well as her resolution of woman's dilemma:

In every government and under every rule, woman has been placed in
a position of slavery—actual, legal slavery. Not perfect slavery, we
grant, not even as perfect a system of slavery even, as our negros; but
still in a very decided state of bondage, inasmuch as she is deprived
of many rights which men enjoy, and legally subjected to the supremacy of man. There is, as a result of such a system, much hardship,
much individual suffering. Many a woman of dominant intellect is
obliged to submit to the rule of an animal in pantaloons, every way
her inferior.[41]

In this first part of a longer extract to follow, both McCord's rhetoric
and analysis of women's historic oppression could be seen, were the
reader to progress no further, as being in perfect concordance with
that of the Grimkés, who would also exclaim that "in all heathen
nations, she has been the slave of man. . . ."[42] It also, of course, would
mesh nicely with the rhetoric of male proslavery promulgators, were
it not for the fact that in the admission of "individual suffering" for
a woman of such "dominant intellect," McCord is surely writing
from a position of personal experience. She even goes on to assert, in
the same essay, that "in individual cases, there may be hardship [for
the negro slave] (though neither as frequently nor as strongly exhib-
ited as in the case of woman) in their fulfilling the necessities of the
position in which circumstances have placed them. . . ." In the second
part of this passage, McCord attempts to ameliorate this dilemma:
"But as we have already remarked, society requires from its members,
on condition of certain advantages accorded, an abandonment of certain rights. Woman has been required to abandon more than man,
because her nature needs more protection. . . . She pays for what she
receives. She needs the arm of a man to defend her against man himself. . . . Equally, and more with the negro, as with the woman, he
needs protection, and must pay for it by the abandonment of privileges which otherwise might seem to be his right."[43] In an argument
echoing William Harper et al., the servitude of both women and
slaves is apparently compensated for in their protection, even though
for McCord the bargain struck seems to be one that weighs more
heavily against the protectees, especially in the case of exceptional
women like herself. And, paradoxically, the male protector is the
same being against whom women need protection, for even more
than the most radical woman's rights advocates, McCord presents an
unflattering image of her male master, that "animal in pantaloons,"
that "thoughtless and often heartless" oppressor.[44]

In many of her essays McCord makes other earnest attempts at finding common ground with Northern woman's right advocates, revealing, in the process, an intricate knowledge of women's historical oppression. (Her own private collection, for whatever reason, included Guilmot's 1852 essay "De la prééminence de la femme sur l'homme"). She agreed, for example, with Sarah Grimké's argument that for the signers of the Declaration of Independence, free and equal was a status to be reserved for white men only, claiming that "our forefathers no more thought of including the negro in their acceptation of the word man, than they were prepared for a similar admission of the word female-man as is now and with equal plausibility claimed by our progressive ladies."[45] Compared to a Northern woman like Catherine Beecher, some of McCord's statements on women even contain a ring of progressivism, especially when viewed against the stereotypes of Southern backwardness. Unlike Beecher, for example, McCord could exclaim that women's duties were not to be "confine[d] to shirtmaking, pudding-mixing, and other such household gear, nor yet even to the adornment of her own fair person," and in her essay "Woman and Her Needs" she admitted that "there is nothing unwomanish in the fullest exercise by woman of the thought and mind, which if God had given, he has given for use." Evidently because she felt hypocritical in admonishing women not to engage in those activities which occupied so much of her own time, she further conceded that "there is nothing unwomanish in the writing of such thoughts; nothing unwomanish even, we think, in the publishing of them."[46] Yet in another context she could turn around and exclaim that "she has no need for the exercise of her intellect" while parenthetically adding "(and woman, we grant, may have a great, a longing, a hungering intellect, equal to man's). . . ."[47] Obviously written from personal experience and her own torment in not being fully able to optimize her own capabilities, McCord was possibly hoping that such advice would protect other women from the same inner conflicts that she had experienced.

Far from being an "undervaluer of woman," McCord could "profess [herself] her advocate" because in her proper sphere woman was morally superior to the male. It was they, the women's rights conveners, who brought women down to an unequal position in that stooping to conquer they became the "petticoated despisers of their sex."[48] Untainted by remaining unexposed to baser masculine traits, woman was not seen by McCord as inferior or unequal to man but rather superior in her feminine moral virtues and, in relative comparison to man, merely "different." And it was in this "beautiful recognition of her unlikeness to man" that her true liberation lay, "the one great truth which must be evolved to make woman no longer the weak plaything of a tyrannic master, no longer the trampled thing, pleading for tolerance at the foot of her conqueror. . . ."[49]

Ultimately, to reduce the coupling of white women with slavery to a mere rhetorical analogy is to trivialize what was for both the Grimké sisters and Louisa McCord a tangible reality, even though they interpreted that reality differently. All three women, after all, had attempted to transgress the nineteenth century's gender boundaries and had encountered the intransigence of male authority across the great divide. Nevertheless, the three also participated in and helped to shape a contested nineteenth-century discourse on the unstable contours of woman's proper sphere, and while they would ultimately draw the boundaries differently, they shared a consensus in recognizing the mighty masculine hand of the master draftsman. While the Grimkés hailed the liberatory potential in the analogy of women and slaves, Louisa McCord could affirm the connection while recognizing all too well the dire consequences of the demise of the plantation system, if not for slaves then certainly for slaveholding women. If women's rights were, as she remarked, "but a piece with negro emancipation," then the abolition of slavery could only mean, as her male proslavery protagonists reminded her, the abolition of her relatively privileged position as well. For after the South's cause was lost, an embittered McCord chose a temporary exodus in Canada rather than submit to the rule of damn Yankees and Negroes. In letters to her son-in-law written during this time, she referred to herself as a "dangerous inmate" and detailed the consequences were she to return to her homeland, for much more so than a man "the presence of an offensive and discontented individual like myself, even though only an old woman, [would] help to draw disagreeable attention."[50] McCord knew that she had no place in the New South; yet unknowingly or not, she was an "inmate" of the Old South also, captive as she was to the region's system of female subordination. And via her writings, McCord may yet be a dangerous inmate for contemporary historians as well, since she still refuses to be confined between the tight spaces of a lined page. Perhaps recognizing that her utility as a writer was spent and that there was no other permissibly public role for such a strong-minded woman, she at one point apparently contemplated suicide, for in another letter to her son-in-law, written while in Canada, she related the story of a neighbor woman of eighty-five who had "deliberately pitched herself headforemost into a well" and remarked that she herself felt "mighty inclined to follow her example."[51] The reader can acknowledge the pain through the pages of the years and still accept that McCord was wrong—at least when it came to her views on slavery. But was she really wrong in her analysis of the intransigence of male supremacy? Perhaps it was later feminists who underestimated its force and were overconfident in believing that formal equality, especially the vote, would be the catalyst of change for women.

That Louisa McCord could concur with the Grimké sisters on the matter of women's transhistorical oppression should not be all that surprising, since she obviously saw through and experienced first-hand the oppressive veil of Southern sexism, however disguised as protective paternalism. She might peek through that veil via her published writings, but to stand unexposed on an equal footing with the male patricians of the South was an impossibility she clearly recognized. The best she could hope for, like her Roman mentor Cornelia in her published drama *Caius Gracchus*, was to "drive. . . back" her "spirit struggles" and to be content with an unassuming role as a backstage extra, ready and willing to take the lead, yet knowing full well that the principal male actors had not only memorized their lines but had written the script as well.[52] As she privately wrote of her alter ego, Cornelia, "The world of action must to her be almost entirely a closed book."[53]

The Work of Gender in the Southern Renaissance

ANNE GOODWYN JONES

In a famous passage from William Faulkner's *Light in August*, Mississippi lawyer Gavin Stephens speculates on the motivations behind Joe Christmas's murder of the spinster Joanna Burden and his escape to the home of defrocked minister Gail Hightower. Most of the people in the community, along with Joe himself, believe Joe is racially mixed. Here are Stephens's words:

> . . . . his blood would not be quiet, . . . It would not be either one or the other, and let his body save itself. Because the black blood drove him first to the negro cabin. And then the white blood drove him out of there, as it was the black blood which snatched up the pistol and the white blood which would not let him fire it. And it was the white blood which sent him to the minister . . . Then I believe that the white blood deserted him for the moment . . . allowing the black to rise in its final moment and make him turn upon that on which he had postulated his hope of salvation. It was the black blood which swept him by his own desire beyond the aid of any man, swept him up into that ecstasy out of a black jungle . . . and then the black blood failed him again. He . . . defied the black blood for the last time, as he had been defying it for thirty years.[1]

These thoughts, though they were commonplace enough in the thirties, seem shockingly racist today. The notion that race determines character, that white blood is good and black blood is evil, is a notion with no currency. We have been schooled in the effects of socialization; we have seen that differences have to do with poverty and hopelessness, not genes and blood. It is even possible today to read this passage from *Light in August* as a deliberate exposé of the ludicrous basis for racial essentialism. To believe that "blood" produces character requires exactly such a tortured and embattled rationale as Stephens gives us here, with black blood advancing and retreating, white blood winning and losing, as though they were in a war of corpuscles. Faulkner exposes its silliness.

But gender essentialism—the belief that gender differences are the result primarily of natural and biological, not social or cultural forces—still holds its own even today. Here is another less familiar passage from *Light in August*; it describes the first sexual encounters of Joanna Burden and Joe Christmas:

> It was as if he struggled physically with another man for an object of no actual value to either, and for which they struggled on principle alone. . . .
>
> "My God," he thought, "it was like I was the woman and she was the man." But that was not right either. Because she had resisted to the very last. But it was not woman resistance . . . she had resisted fair. . . "I'll show her," he said aloud. . . . He began to tear at her clothes . . . though his hands were hard and urgent it was with rage alone. "At least I have made a woman of her at last," he thought.[2]

In this passage, there is no reference to "womanblood" and "manblood" in mortal combat. Gender is not quite as close to nature for Joe as race was to nature for Gavin Stephens, nor is Joe as close to essentialism as Gavin. What is powerful and painful about the passage is the intensity of Joe's anxiety and rage at a woman who acts like a man. Because there are only two opposed choices for Joe, man or woman, Joanna's acting like a man makes him feel like a woman. And his solution to this unsettling feeling is physical violence: penetrating her body in an act of rape, he "makes a woman of her at last." If culture allows women to take on masculine characteristics, nature can be called on to enforce a biological understanding of gender. Now that she has been "violated," penetrated, made "hollow" as Faulkner writes in *Absalom, Absalom!*, she has been forcibly written back into femininity. Her body will now determine her behavior, Joe believes, just as, in Gavin Stephen's view, black or white blood will determine Joe's.

Questioning southern racial ideology has been a preoccupation of Southern literature and literary criticism for some time. Questioning gender ideology has been less visible, both in the literature and in the criticism. Faulkner, along with a number of other writers during the Southern Renaissance between the two World Wars, used narrative to ask fundamental questions about traditional gender arrangements as well as racial ones, to suggest that gender might be a product of socialization more than of biology, and to lift the exclusionary boundaries that divided human characteristics along a gender divide. This revolution in gender ideology, a revolution that was by no means confined to the South, took on special intensity there, where rigid gender boundaries had always been part of a network of racial and class boundaries as well. To shake the pedestal, or even more disturbing, to refuse the phallus, was to put the entire structure of Southern thinking at risk. Joe's insistence on sculpting Joanna's body with his penis, on reconstructing a natural and seamless relation between body and character, biology and gender, comes out of the same anxiety that he has about his race: without strict categories of identity, he feels, like much of the South, lost and helpless.

I want to begin by dissecting my title. I will start by lopping off the last two words, the Southern Renaissance, then carve into the center with "gender," and end by examining what is left over: the word "work." After the dissection, I will suture the parts, keeping them in the same order. I will then discuss briefly the history of gender in the period of the Southern Renaissance. And I will conclude with a quick survey of some fictions produced during this period that offered new ways of thinking about gender.

Not everyone confines the Southern Renaissance between the World Wars, but it is certainly safe to start there. The Southern Renaissance—sometimes spelled "Renascence"—generally is taken to refer to the blossoming of southern intellectual life after the First World War, signalled most clearly by the name William Faulkner. It may be odd to call it a renaissance rather than a naissance, a rebirth rather than a birth, for a search for the first coming of southern intellectual life takes us down some troubled paths.

The Southern Renaissance traditionally has been limited to literary production. But as Daniel Singal, Michael O'Brien, and Richard King have shown us, this gives a distorted and limiting view of the period. In Chapel Hill sociologists thrived under the direction of

Howard Odum; the University of North Carolina Press published challenging and provocative books on the South. In Nashville, meanwhile, the Fugitive poets turned political and produced *I'll Take My Stand*, a collection of passionate essays arguing for a more conservative vision of the South as the stronghold of agrarianism against the onslaught of industrialism. In other urban (or proto-urban) centers across the South, from New Orleans to Charleston to Richmond, the new generation of white Southerners created literary and intellectual magazines, while journalist Wilbur Cash in Charlotte wrote his deeply felt analysis of the mind of the South.

Now it is becoming clear that even the literary canon of the Southern Renaissance needs to be revised. The typical Southern literature text includes poets and novelists and literary theorists, such as Allen Tate, John Crowe Ransom, Robert Penn Warren, Ellen Glasgow, Katherine Anne Porter, Caroline Gordon, and, of course, William Faulkner. Any new anthology will need to include a much more diverse group of writers—women such as Frances Newman, Evelyn Scott, and Elizabeth Madox Roberts; politically radical novelists such as Fielding Burke and Myra Page; and Southern black poets and novelists typically thought of in the context of the Harlem Renaissance, such as Richard Wright, Zora Neale Hurston, and Anne Spencer.

The endpoint of the Southern Renaissance is yet another point of scholarly contention: some say it has never ended, that we are still in it. My own sense is that the changes brought by the Second World War to the South were vast and deep enough to suggest a break early in the 1940s; the literature of the war years and of the postwar period should be thought of in different and more national and international contexts. I am defining the Southern Renaissance both inclusively, to capture within its net as wide a range as possible of Southern-born and Southern-raised writers and, exclusively, to include only the period between the World Wars.

Now let us carve out the second term, "gender." Here I want to clarify that I am using gender to describe not biological differences that have to do primarily with reproduction—which I am calling sex—but historical differences that have to do with attitudes and behavior. I take the view that gender can be useful as a term that, in its difference from sex, helps us to see more clearly the changes over time in what it means to be a man or a woman, and hence the constructed or cultural basis for, and thus the mutability of, our own gender identities.

Finally, "work." What could I possibly mean by "the work of gen-

der"? To answer this I need to turn to a theory of ideology. Sacvan
Bercovitch has defined ideology as "the system of interlinked ideas,
symbols, and beliefs by which a culture—any culture—seeks to justify and perpetuate itself; the web of rhetoric, ritual, and assumption
through which society coerces, persuades, and coheres."[3] Ideology
works because it feels like common sense; it is the mental equivalent
to the air we breathe, and nearly as invisible. A typically successful
strategy of ideology is to distinguish what is natural from what is
unnatural: heterosexuality is natural, homosexuality is unnatural; in-
traracial marriage is natural, interracial marriage is unnatural. Further, ideology is not arbitrary; it produces belief systems—indeed, it
produces people—who are appropriate to given material conditions.
Changed material conditions require changed ideology. In order to
run the factories during the war, Rosie the Riveter had to be imagined;
in order to provide jobs for GIs when they returned, she had to be told
that working was unfeminine and bad for her kids, i.e., unnatural. To
make the two-income family possible, we had to have a middle-class
women's liberation movement.

In *Male Subjectivity at the Margins*, Kaja Silverman argues that
ideology works at the level of belief, prior to consciousness and
knowledge, the level at which we construct our sense of reality itself.
This sense of reality she calls the "dominant fiction."[4] The word
"dominant" calls attention both to the power of this belief and to the
presence of alternative beliefs which it dominates. The word "fiction" calls attention to the changeability of this belief over time and
place; it is always a fiction, but when it is dominant, people believe
it is true. These are frightening ideas, because they call into question
the very notion of reality. But they are at the same time liberating
because they point to our capacity for invention and change. Silverman argues that the American "dominant fiction" has rested on
the fundamental equation of the phallus, the signifier of power (especially as articulated by Jacques Lacan), with the penis, which signifies
masculinity. We believe that men are powerful and women are not, in
ways that extend far beyond biology. Silverman's effort is to show how,
by revising ideology, or belief, we can reshape human possibilities and
human history. If the phallus can be exposed as a fiction, and the
identification of the phallus and penis called into question, then we
can think about human power and potential in more diverse and intricate ways. The "work of gender," then, can reproduce the status quo
by reaffirming the equation of phallus and penis, or revise it by challenging that identification. In the second passage quoted earlier from

Light in August, Joe Christmas tries forcibly to reassert the identification of the penis and phallus. Watching Joanna act "like a man" has for Joe threatened the dominant fiction; his work of gender is to reinstate it.

A couple of examples of the work of gender in the American South: in the antebellum South, proslavery apologists argued for an organic society in which each category of being had its proper place. The point was to justify slavery, but gender played its part, for women belonged below the patriarch in the hierarchy, along with blacks and children. Gender constructions of women as essentially different from men justified their inferior place. Even women agreed with this ideology; Louisa McCord, an intellectual white woman, argued against giving women the vote on the grounds that women should not be subjected without protection to the physical superiority and possible violence of men. Her gender construction worked to preserve patriarchal power even as it chastised men—what can a woman do but placate men, if they are stronger?

Again, during the period of Jim Crow, the image of the African-American man as black beast rapist took hold of the popular imagination. This gender construction of black masculinity depended on and worked in tandem with the continuing image of white women as physically frail and in need of protection by white men. Together these gender constructions worked to reinforce both white and male supremacy.

These are explicit ideological statements of gender definitions; they can be found stated baldly as such in newspapers, magazines, sermons, essays, and represented through characters' voices in novels. A more difficult question has to do with the effects of such explicit efforts. Did they accomplish what they set out to do, that is, enforce a "savage ideal" of gender conformity? No. For one thing, the dominant ideology, as we saw, is rarely, if ever, the only ideology that circulates. In the South, for example, African gender traditions persisted, and class produced differing ideas of manhood and womanhood. In addition to these alternative ideologies of gender, we need to consider the effects of family and personality differences on gender norms. Some individuals, like the Grimké sisters from Charleston, will resist the norm; some, like Louisa McCord, will revise it even as they claim to be supporting the norm.

Imaginative literature is an unusually useful place to look if one is interested in ideological questions. Whatever its conventions—romance, realism, naturalism, modernism—poetry, and especially fiction, represents reality in some way. Rather than directly mouthing ideology, fiction typically gives us a character or a narrator within a fictional world that requires interpretation. Instead of looking at ideological statements in isolation, the novel places them within the fiction of a historical context. Just as the historian might look not only at gender pronouncements at a given time and place, but also at their effects and meanings for historical people, so the literary critic analyzes explicit ideological claims within the fiction's context. And just as a historian might locate gender ideology (and resistance to it) in places more subtle than explicit claims—for example, in wills, or court records, or diaries—so the literary critic examines the more subtle ways in which the text represents and contests its explicit claims. A case in point is white lawyer Gavin Stephens's claims about Joe Christmas's blood, in *Light in August*. We need to see this speech as telling us more about Stephens and his class at the time than about the novel's position on racial difference. To accept such a statement as explanatory for the novel is to miss the world in which Faulkner placed it, and to miss, therefore, the meanings of that world.

When we look at literature, then, we want to be subtle and imaginative, to read the signs with care, and to be aware that a single novel might contain the dominant ideology or fiction, alternative ideologies, and idiosyncratic inventions and resistances. If the work of gender is to organize people's minds to suit their material conditions, then we can in certain fictions watch gender at work.

The Southern Renaissance was a time when more play was allowed into the work of gender, when alternative and resistant constructions of gender were able to be imagined and narrated. Seen as the pinnacle of Southern writing for reasons of high productivity, high quality, formal experimentation, and links to international modernism, the Southern Renaissance—both the fictions and the nonfiction—should also be seen as a primary locus for the representation of and enactment of the works of genders in the South between the wars. Southern literature can, therefore, provide historians with a place to begin and return to, in developing understandings of Southern gender in this period; moreover, a focus on gender in these texts can offer literary critics a new way of reading not only individual works, such as *Light in August,* but also new ways of reading the Southern Renaissance as a whole.

The history of gender in the twentieth-century South has not yet been written, although studies such as Jacquelyn Hall's *Revolt against Chivalry* represent major steps toward understanding certain groups of Southern women at certain moments. Even less has been done on the history of men and manhood in the twentieth-century South; the last pages of Ted Ownby's *Subduing Satan* only begin to address the question. But it is possible to look at histories of modern American gender and then use histories of the modern South (though not specifically of gender) to speculate about gender in the South. And it is possible for a scholar of culture to read the tea leaves of literature for signs of that history.

In his splendid history of modern American sex roles, *Him/Her/ Self*, Peter Filene confines himself to a study of the middle class as that class (here he quotes David Riesman) whose "opinions shift and which is therefore largely responsible for fluctuations in cultural and political tendencies."[5] However valid his rationale, such a focus would be a Procrustean bed for the gangly South, with its rural traditions, its slow move to urban corporate life-styles, and its multiracial cultures. Nevertheless, Filene's arguments provide an extremely useful template against which Southern differences can be made visible.

Most scholars agree with Filene that the First World War brought a domestic revolution in sex roles. The disillusionments with the war were massive and deep; they extended to disillusionment with the entire structure of values that seemed to support the war effort. Betrayed by their forebears, young men and women—those born around the turn of the century—felt a gulf between the generations and acted out their rebellion in forms of behavior, including sexual and gender behavior, to their parents' horror.

Complicating the question for young women was the history of feminism to this point. Their role models, the women who had pushed through suffrage in 1920, advocated a sort of feminism that drew upon explicit ideology—ideologies of equality, pushed by the Women's Party in the ERA, and ideologies of work as joy and duty, pushed by more conservative groups. Neither of these ideologies adequately addressed what seemed to be more personal and private concerns, such as sexual pleasure, or freedom to travel or play or shop without masculine constraint. The flapper emerged as the Twenties' answer both to the end of the Victorian values of the patriarchy and to the idealistic (and perhaps also Victorian) values of radical feminism. The flapper, with her bobbed hair, her short, fringed skirt, and her explicit pleasure in sex (whether intercourse or near it), leapt into the fountains at the Plaza Hotel in New York holding her glass of champagne, horrifying her elders, and pleasing her friends, the embodiment of what Filene calls a "revised version" of feminism.[6]

Surely it is no coincidence that the first, and most famous, flapper was a Southerner. Scott Fitzgerald met Zelda Sayre when he was stationed in Alabama during the First World War; he married her and took her into a now-fabled life, in New York, New England, and Europe, a life that epitomized the flaming youth and wild excesses of the Twenties. As a Southern woman, Zelda did not inherit a history of feminism. The closest thing to it, the movement for suffrage in the South—despite wide participation and such well-known leaders as Ellen Glasgow in Virginia—was implicated all too frequently with the drive to retain white supremacy and class structures. As had Louisa McCord at the time of the first women's movement before the Civil War, intellectual women of the twentieth-century South used their minds to oppose women's equality on the grounds of their vulnerability to male violence. Any intellectual tradition of feminism in the South had to be traced to the sisters who left it—the Grimkés, Angelina and Sarah—or worked out not on constitutional but on biblical grounds, as twentieth-century interracial activists such as Katherine DuPre Lumpkin would find. The South, long resistant to abstractions of any kind, particularly those imposed from outside, was not fertile ground for Northern liberal or radical feminism.

But this is precisely the feminism that died, or went underground, with the Twenties. And the Twenties revolution in gender addressed issues that were all too familiar to white southern women: women's bodies, women's voices, women's submission to patriarchal family, and community control. These concerns were personal, private, and nonabstract. They were what the nation seemed to want after the First World War, and, not for the first time, it turned to the South for its narrative. Ideology as narrative found exactly its representative in Southerner Zelda Sayre Fitzgerald.

In the South, white women's bodies, voices, and control had long been linchpins to an elaborate ideological structure linking gender with race and class. The body of the privileged white woman was revered as a marble statue, a Grecian urn, a human body that by nature resembled the finest productions of masculine art. As such, it needed protection from vandals; as such, it had nothing inside, no desires or will: its identity was constituted by absence, hollowness waiting to be filled. Of course, no one literally embodied this image, but it informed the imaginations and set the expectations of all Southerners to some extent. First, for white men, this image implied the purity of blood and thus of white patriarchal lineage: white supremacy a well as the male line of succession and inheritance were guaranteed by her chastity and desirelessness. This was particularly crucial since no such behavior characterized white men; on the contrary, their desiring black women and enforcing that desire was visibly producing a lighter race. Dividing women into categories—black and white, lady and woman—was one way to maintain a sense of control; enforcing these categories through the pleasures of privilege and as forms of identity guaranteed cooperation from its targets. The white woman's fragility further guaranteed her distance from earthy interests and gave the man an opportunity to construct his own manhood in protecting her. Finally, class distinctions could be maintained by etherealizing privilege: the earthier the woman, the stronger, and the lower class. Yet white male cross-class bonding could be sustained by continually stroking their shared bonds of white racial superiority and masculine authority over women, earthy or angelic. White patriarchal families lay at the center of southern social organization; and white families were ideologically preserved by this image of the frail, pure, desireless, submissive woman. In practice, of course, such a woman would have been an unutterable bore, and the struggles were more complicated. Yet patriarchal authority over women's bodies, voices, and freedom remained the *sine qua non*, however fiery and rebellious the woman. What Zelda and the flapper did, then, was to begin to challenge this notion. Privileged white women—daughters of judges, like Zelda and Faulkner's Temple Drake—expressed sexual and other desires and demands, blurring the boundaries of race and class, unleashing the specter of loss of male control over paternity, threatening the foundation of male strength on female weakness and male dominance on female submission. Despite Zelda's compromised and tragic marriage and life, her early image was one that challenged the national idea of womanhood by turning Southern norms upside down.

The national needs for a new gender for women that swerved away from pietistic abstractions and grounded itself in issues involving the control of the woman's body and desires thus found satisfaction in the South. The regional and national traditions merged at this cultural juncture. But the same does not seem to have been the case for white manhood. Nationally, middle class men—like women—recoiled from Victorian high sentiments and values. But whereas the women saw continuity and expansion in their roles—adding paying work to domestic, expecting to have personal desires addressed—men saw primarily loss. Filene's middle-class men found themselves, in the Twenties, caught up in jobs that gave them little authority and control, pushing paper and products as salesmen of various stripes, Babbitts confused between manipulating images and retaining Victorian integrity, and confronted with women who seemed to be demanding more of what they were increasingly less able to give. Such men turned to culture heroes in sports, or men like Lindbergh, or—in the Depression—Franklin Delano Roosevelt, to find identifications. Stunned by the war's effects, they had rejected the Victorian patriarch as a model but now floundered without adequate alternatives; giving up dominance seemed too close to accepting submission.

Such a description does not seem likely to work well for Southern white men's experiences and gender struggles during the period. The premise, the spread of corporate urban and suburban life, can be found only spottily in the still largely rural and agricultural South. The loss of patriarchal identity took different forms in the South, some long in the making.

Southern white manhood had had a different history from manhood elsewhere in the nation. Partly constructed by prescriptive ideology in the service of the slavery debates, and partly the construct of longer histories of masculinity as personal honor, Southern white manhood had developed along differing lines. Victorian patriarchal appeals to character in the North developed out of an ethic of conscience, of interiority; Victorian patriarchal appeals to honor in the South developed, as Bertram Wyatt-Brown has so persuasively shown, out of an ethic of public reputation, of exteriority.[7] Manhood in the South was a matter of constant creation and re-creation; the site for such creativity was typically a community of other white men. Whether in eye-gouging contests on the frontier or sophisticated duels in the plantation South, Southern men subjected their bodies to man-making, and unmaking, physical contests. Of course honor took other, less tangible, forms as well; yet, the presence of the body in these contests suggests the personal, individual nonabstract location of masculinity in the South, as well as its continual vulnerability to contestation.

Clearly there are links between this history of personal, often physically and violently produced manhood, and the system of slavery that depended on the power of violence, or, more precisely, the belief in the power of white male violence to survive. What is striking to me is what seems to have happened to white men's sexuality as this ideology of manhood worked itself out. Especially in the late nineteenth century and early twentieth century, white men—like black men—were ideologically laden with sexuality. And their sexuality was laced with, and indistinguishable from, violence: the black beast rapist was born out of the merging of myths of black sexuality, black violence, white female vulnerability, and white female desirelessness. Such an image—the black beast rapist—rationalized white manhood as the protector of women and the enforcer of white supremacy, and thus of civilization itself. But what it also did— together with the images of black and white women already discussed—was eliminate the ideological space for white men's sexuality.

Although there is no doubt that white southern men practiced and enjoyed their sexuality whatever the circumstances, Southern ideology, and to a certain extent Southern practice, had directed it along lines that could not be articulated as ideology. The "paths to the back yard" that Lillian Smith described, echoing Mary Chesnut's bitterness of nearly a century before, point to one such silenced practice: the use of black women for sex, and its denial before white women.[8] The ascription of excessive, and thus in some senses superior, sexuality to black men, the nonnarrated practice of sex with black women, and the constantly narrated veneration of white women's purity, left a vacuum where white male sexual prowess might have appeared. This was not inconsistent with general Victorian notions about male sexuality; what was different in the South was its implicit comparison to black virility. White men were left without a plausible narrative of their own sexuality. Their response, as I see it, was to displace that sexuality onto a discourse of "penetration." In this discourse, manhood and dominance were coded into acts of penetration—whether literally, through gouging, dueling, or wounding, or figuratively, as in entering a door, a family, or a class. Conversely, being penetrated was the sign of effeminization: to be vulnerable at one's boundaries, to be unable to defend against invasion, was to be humiliated and feminized. Manhood came to be defined not in relation or opposition to womanhood and women, but between and among men. Hence the signs or markers of masculinity and femininity became markers of relative manhood among men more significantly than they were markers of difference between men and women. However, there was a catch to this rationale: in order to stabilize the system, women had to remain stable, unchanged, in place and recognizable as female, the measure against which manhood could be measured, the distance from which determined one's masculinity. In short, women had to remain submissive, not dominant, penetrable, not penetrating.

Invasion and penetration by the Yankees, both in the Civil War and in the stages of Reconstruction, was inevitably, then, a form of feminization for white Southern men. Surrender and loss clinched the identification. But this identification of Southern white manhood with the feminine antedates the War: Northern stereotypes of Southern men ascribed to them such feminine qualities as impulsiveness, emotionality, proximity to nature rather than culture, and lack of trained intelligence. Here is a famous description of Rooney Lee, Robert E. Lee's son, from Henry Adams's *Education:* "He was simple beyond analysis. . . . No one knew enough to know how ignorant he was; how childlike; how helpless before the relative complexity of a school. As an animal the Southerner seemed to have every advantage, but even as an animal he steadily lost ground. . . . Strictly, the Southerner had no mind; he had temperament. . . ."⁹ And insofar as national discourses identified the masculine and the North with coldness, efficiency, work, and the urban life, Southern men were willing to accept the implicit charge of femininity when it appeared within a discourse that characterized the South as a site of warmth, leisure, pleasure, and intimacy with nature.

It is not surprising, then, to find that Southern white men of the period between the wars struggled with manhood and masculinity on somewhat different terms from those of their non-Southern peers. Where, as Filene suggests, the First World War failed to deliver on its promise to restore masculinity to American men, Southern men took that promise more seriously and in some cases found what it offered—not only a renewal of masculinity, but a chance to restore the military honor lost in the Civil War. Whereas Northern middle-class men looked for heroes in contemporary culture—sports, flight, national politics—Southern men found them in the Civil War past and on the local political scene. While Northern middle-class men feared the loss of strenuous manhood to urban constraints, Southern men had no such fear, and continued to hunt, fish, farm, and drink. And Southerners, to an extent more pervasive than Northerners, constructed their manhood on a daily basis of racial difference.

Such is the setting—speculative though it is—within which Southern white men and women wrote out their perceptions and prescriptions for gender. The novels of Southern women confirm our sense that the revision of gender for women was part of a national movement away from political, abstract claims and into the ostensibly personal and private. The novels of Southern men suggest a different agenda from the national preoccupations of manhood at the time.

Women novelists told new stories of female sexuality and desire, of resistance to patriarchal traditions and practices, of finding a voice. Men, in contrast, struggled to find ways to sustain continuity in patriarchal power while allowing for crucial changes in traditional masculinity and addressing the changes in women. Their stories of the new New Woman, the liberated woman of the Twenties, are ambivalent, as one might expect, but finally seem to reveal more of anxiety than delight. This new Southern woman with her voice, her control over her body and sexuality, and her explicit resistance to patriarchy, is too risky to retain in the stories of anxious manhood that characterize the Southern Renaissance.

Among women, writing about desire arguably began as early as 1899 when Kate Chopin wrote *The Awakening*, an incendiary story of a young married woman and mother whose infatuation for an unmarried man parallels her growth into autonomy. Chopin took an even more radical step by having her protagonist, Edna Pontellier, experience sexual pleasure outside the bounds not only of marriage but also of romantic love, for she has an affair with another man whose attraction is simply sensual. We last see Edna Pontellier as she sinks down, drowning in the Gulf, unable to find a way to reconcile her discoveries with her community. Novelists of the Southern Renaissance found a place, however difficult, for their new New Women to survive. With their desires and their voices and their resistances to patriarchal control, Frances Newman's shocking novels of the Twenties—*The Hard-Boiled Virgin* and *Dead Lovers Are Faithful Lovers*—tell the story first of a woman whose sexuality is complicated by her sense of theater and desire to write, and then of two women who passionately love the same man. Katherine Anne Porter challenged the stereotypes of Southern women in her Miranda stories, showing women pushing at the boundaries of cultural definition, claiming desire and autonomy, and finding a voice. Elizabeth Madox Roberts began her important novel, *The Time of Man*, with the voice of Ellen Chesser, writing her own name in the air. Ellen Glasgow in *Barren Ground* showed readers a woman whose desire is betrayed and who turns instead to her work, becoming the most respected and successful and fertile farmer in the area. Margaret Mitchell pit two types of female desire against one another, showing both Scarlett's erotic attraction to the feminized Ashley Wilkes and her more stereotypical sexuality aroused by Rhett Butler's masculine force. Zora Neale Hurston rewarded Janie, in *Their Eyes Were Watching God*, with the perfect lover—young, gorgeous, playful, and sensitive—after Janie signifies on her patriarchal husband's private parts. These audacious stories have in common the reclaiming of women's bodies and women's desires. Access to desire means access to creativity and voice; access to voice means a way to resist patriarchal command. Yet in each narrative, women's desire is complicated: by relationships to children, to other women, to husbands and lovers; and by conflicting narratives of desire's production, in a scene of love or violence, pleasure or intimacy.

Southern men writing during this period also represented this new New Woman, the woman with desire, a voice, autonomy. Predictably, though, however complex their responses, men tended to see little to be gained and much to be feared from this change. Masculinity seemed hard enough to deal with, especially after the First World War; now women were removing the stability that had given manhood a compass point, a true north. Allen Tate's character Lacy Buchan feels anxiety about women's bodies anywhere below the neck, and sometimes above it. The novel begins with burial of Lacy's mother. Later, the young girl he loves is sent to a convent after an attempted rape, and his sister goes mad. Lacy becomes a soldier and remains a bachelor. Faulkner's *The Unvanquished* shows Bayard Sartoris rewriting masculinity in crucial ways, defying the history of violence and bloodshed that had defined his father and ushering in a time of peace and a new sort of manhood. Unfortunately, it is at the cost of his sexuality, for Drusilla, to whom he is evidently attracted, leaves the narrative, having lost control of the story itself to Bayard. Elsewhere, Faulkner's more feminine men—the Ashley Wilkes sorts, the poets and thinkers—run the risk of retreating into an airy transcendence where no bodies live. Or, like Horace Benbow and Joe Christmas, they find themselves trapped and overwhelmed by the force of the desiring female body. Manly men fare no better; the World War I pilot in *Flags in the Dust* is obsessed not with his dead wife but with his dead brother and cannot feel comfortable except among men. Meanwhile, Faulkner's liberated heroine Linda Snopes has a voice like a duck, and Joe rewards Joanna Burden's voice by cutting her throat. There is trouble with female desire in men's texts as well as in women's, but it is a very different kind of trouble.

During the Southern Renaissance, then, writers from the most canonized to the most obscure carried on the cultural work of revising gender. As women found new ground and focus for their identities, locating them within rather than outside the woman's body, men simultaneously explored new possibilities for manhood yet reacted with anxiety to the new freedom of women. Perhaps it was too much, too soon; certainly there was an air both of giddiness and of terror for all concerned. Yet, their experiments with gender were as serious as their experiments with racial boundaries and with modernist fictional form. After all, any rewriting of gender in the form of narrative must take as an assumption that culture, rather than nature, constructs gender itself. Otherwise writing could make no difference at all. The work of these women and men with gender thus deserves to become visible as a major component of and contributor to the Southern Renaissance.

The Desperate Imagination:

Writers and Melancholy in the Modern American South

BERTRAM WYATT-BROWN

Ever since the early nineteenth century, when Southerners discovered that they inhabited a distinctive region, their literature has differed in important ways from that of the rest of the country. That distinctiveness included a preoccupation with the ethic of honor, a sentiment and code with which Northerners had only a fast fading acquaintance. Southern letters were also touched by the same specters of melancholy that shade most of western cultural life. Yet, because of defeat in civil war, hostile race relations, and a sense of economic, political, and intellectual inferiority, romantic alienation—about which western literature has long been concerned—took deeper root in Southern soil than it did elsewhere in the nation. Moreover, the code itself encouraged men to represent themselves as figures of manly perfection; those unable to meet that criterion sometimes found themselves the object of suspicion, ridicule, or even violence.

Dread of shame and failure to meet their own or the community's expectations might drive some to despair and isolation. As Anthony Storr, the British psychoanalyst, has observed, a chief feature of artists with depressive tendencies is "the fragility of their self-esteem." To avoid public disgrace—as they interpret any slight or criticism—

they "compensate for inner emptiness" through creative work—and sometimes overwork.[1] For Southern women of sensitivity and high intelligence, to fall short of such feminine ideals as beauty, submissiveness, fertility in marriage, and modest reserve was a frequent source of agony.[2] In the interwar period of the twentieth century the old ethical standards were losing their significance, but Southern letters still reflected much of their spirit.

In 1945 Allen Tate illuminated Southern exceptionalism when he explained why, in the years between the two great wars, an outpouring of regional fiction and poetry far exceeded the quality of prior literary generations. In a quotation often cited, Tate argued, "With the war of 1914–1918, the South reentered the world but gave a backward glance as it stepped over the border," a retrospection, he continued, that furnished the nation with a "literature conscious of the past in the present."[3] In that era of political and social upheaval, he contended, the writer's imagination found fertile soil for intellectual growth.[4] Although he did not realize it, Tate, as well as critics who followed his lead, was describing a psychological phenomenon and not a purely sociological one. "That backward glance," that nostalgia for a time shrouded in a haze of legend, was a form of mourning. Just as the interwar writers' forebears made the Lost Cause a sacred commemoration, so did such writers as William Faulkner and others of his generation grieve the erosion of old ideals and decry their generation's failure to unearth a source of faith to replace them. Literary critic Lewis Simpson has elegantly expanded on Tate's theme, calling the South of the literary imagination "the dispossessed garden."[5] But he and others have not carried their metaphors of lost innocence and remembrance of things past far enough. The theme of deep estrangement had a psychological dimension in the regional culture. Mourning, depression, and their sometime consort, mania, also affected individual writers whose lives—and deaths—will help to explain the special nature of Southern letters.

Bearing in mind the complex mingling of anger, guilt, shame, and love that comprise the mourning process, four themes are examined, ones that highlight the interrelationship of life and art in such particularly melancholy writers as William Styron, William Faulkner, Katherine Anne Porter, Evelyn Scott, Carson McCullers, Truman Capote, Tennessee Williams, and others. By understanding the ways in which art and psychological biography come together, we can better apprehend the ambivalent nature of Southern longing for the old times to which Tate alluded. The late Melvin Bradford put the question of Southern nostalgia in a positive frame, calling it the "elegiac wisdom" of Southern letters.[6] First, the sense of communal loss that marked Tate's generation had its parallel in the lives of the writers themselves. A substantial number of interwar writers suffered from chronic despair to greater or lesser degree, sometimes with origins in biological inheritance. Obviously those artists sunk in the deepest wells of hopelessness can compose nothing worthwhile, but when the inner void and misery disappear and rationality returns—as it generally does—they find in the urge to write a means of handling the experience. "I believe you have to discover your true self through ordeal," the late Walker Percy once exclaimed. "It helps enormously when a person can make a friend with her terror, plumb the depths of her depression. 'There's gold down there in the darkness,' said Dr. Jung."[7] Second, this correlation between the regional culture and its literary vanguard can be traced to the antebellum period, when a cult of Byronic disenchantment furnished the isolated and often inconsolable planter intellectuals with some means, largely private, to express their moody dissatisfactions. Third, the twentieth-century Southern intellectuals found precedent and inspiration in those European and Northern writers whose works revealed a similar sense of existential doubt and personal affliction. Literary critic Louis Rubin speculates, for instance, that perhaps "without Joyce's novel [Ulysses] there might never have been The Sound and the Fury."[8] In the South the weakening of the old order, with its patriarchal customs and simple convictions, and the opening of pathways to new literary approaches separated the interwar group from the regional writers of the preceding era. Fourth, in translating these fresh perspectives and inward-gazing forms into their own idiom, Southern writers, by their exertions, gladly purchased temporary relief from the ghosts that had haunted their lives from an early age. Yet, tragically for some, the mental infirmity or complications derived from it gradually strangled the will to exercise their craft. Making matters worse was the inclination of some Southern artists to follow the self-destructive dictates of Dionysus and Bacchus. Plato had noted the failing among poets more than two thousand years ago. Although still a matter of medical controversy, mania, depression, and compulsive drinking are, in actuality, interrelated problems.[9] The losing battle against uncontrollable inner forces left them pale and shaken, awaiting death.

At the outset, melancholia must be differentiated from the ordinary ups and downs of existence that all human beings experience. As Kathleen Woodward reminds us, "Our lives are shaped and reshaped by losses which are succeeded by restitution."[10] When such adversities occur early in life, however, the child has no adequate means for dealing with feelings of anger, guilt, and sense of betrayal. The problems of repression and torment are likely to reappear in later years when similar losses occur.[11] Aware of his own inherited inclination to depression and knowing early maternal loss, William Styron, whose *Lie Down in Darkness* immediately identified him as a leading Southern novelist, has elaborated on the wretchedness to which the alienated child and man may surrender. "In depression," he wrote on the occasion of Primo Levi's suicide in 1988, "the sick brain plays evil tricks on its inhabiting spirit. Slowly overwhelmed by the struggle, the intellect blurs into stupidity. All capacity for pleasure disappears, and despair maintains a merciless daily drumming."[12]

Critics such as Louis Rubin deny that there is any correlation between the kind of malady that Styron describes and the creative impulse. In a denunciation of psychoanalytic interpretation, Rubin declares: "What the assumption leaves out is that great art is distinguished by its powers of control and synthesis, of making the disparate and disjointed experience of life into that which is unified and whole: by its shaping form. This is precisely what the neurotic person is *unable* to do."[13] In an interview as early as 1954 Styron challenged the popular misapprehension that Rubin voiced: "The good writing of any age has always been the product of *someone's* neurosis, and we'd have a mighty dull literature if all the writers that came along were a bunch of happy chuckleheads."[14] Likewise, Carson McCullers, whose first novel, *The Heart Is a Lonely Hunter*, in 1940 propelled her into national fame, once made the same point: "One cannot explain accusations of morbidity. A writer can only say he writes from the seed which flowers later in the subconscious. Nature is not abnormal, only lifelessness is abnormal." McCullers, who was afflicted with physical disabilities and wracking pain, knew also the depths of despair. Her marriage to an alcoholic aggravated her own drinking habits.[15]

We find such a pattern, for instance, in novelist Truman Capote's elders, whose number included several family members with emotional problems, from alcoholism to agoraphobia. Sometimes an inherited predisposition to mental illness lay behind a writer's unhappy state of mind. The two-hundred-year old clan that produced Walker Percy and his cousin William Alexander Percy, author of *Lanterns on the Levee*, included several men who committed suicide and a series of Percys, both men and women, who suffered from chronic melancholia.[16] Capote himself was stricken with "recurrent depression that dogged him like a nagging cold," declared one of his lovers.[17] We find a similar instance in the biography of Tennessee Williams, who reported his relief at never having had children because "there have been too many instances of extreme eccentricity and even lunacy in my family on all four sides." His puritanical and eventually paranoid mother used to scream loud enough for the children to hear whenever she and her husband were having sex. The youngsters were terrified and used to run to the neighbors—or so Williams claimed. After years of increasing madness, Williams's beloved sister Rose underwent the torture of a lobotomy. Rose and Tennessee's mother, Edwina, hoped that the operation would stop Roses's gross sexual comments. With reference to a pioneer of the Southern Renaissance, Ellen Glasgow, who once was almost a suicide herself, had a brother who successfully carried out that mission at age thirty-nine.[18]

Genetics and neurological complications, however, cover only a fraction of the cases. Much more common among writers of downcast temperament is an early deprivation of parental love. Sometimes death snatched one parent or both away, but more often the children were emotionally rather than physically deserted, with mordant effects on the future artist. Indeed, it is hard to find a single major author in the South—or elsewhere—whose childhood was not traumatic or at least lonely and sad. William Styron's father, a talented naval engineer, fell into black moods or a "thick cloud of rage" that filled the house and left the son frightened and forlorn.[19] Evelyn Scott, the Tennessee novelist, was reared in an even more pervasive atmosphere of gloom and conflict in Clarksville. Her parents were a disastrous mismatch. Seely Dunn, her father, came from Northern, carpetbag extraction, and her mother prided herself on aristocratic Southern roots allegedly stretching back on one side to Irish royalty. During her adolescence, Evelyn complained of parental neglect: "The love of those among whom one had been reared is usually not love at all. One can die inwardly without any of them being aware of it." Having lost the family's wealth in ill-advised business deals in the 1910s and 20s, the parents lived a life that a biographer calls "existential suicide," ending finally in divorce.[20] Such experiences in the youth of a future artist as talented as the long-neglected Evelyn Scott attest to her resilience rather than to the weakness of human response.

Another female author with a childhood of tragedy and sorrow was Katherine Anne Porter of Hays County in eastern Texas. Despite her lifelong fantasies of an aristocratic lineage, she was born to poor but well educated parents. Alice Jones Porter, her mother, became overstrained from caring for an ill-tempered and self-indulgent husband and died in childbirth before Katherine reached the age of two. About that time, the child also lost three nurturing aunts in quick succession. All her life the writer could not escape bouts of lingering dejection. She often wondered, writes her biographer, "if these states had their origin in the early tragedies she could not remember." Often enough, traumas occurring before the arrival of speech can find expression only in fantasy and dreams.[21] Aggrieved over the loss of the gentle Alice, Katherine found no comfort in her relationship with her father, Harrison Porter. In a persistent state of hopelessness and rage, he cruelly belittled the youngsters and, unable to hold a job for long, never provided the family with a decent living. Years later she wrote Annie Gay, her sister, that she was "mystified by his cold attitude toward us, towards life . . . so death-like and despairing and inert and will-less."[22] As a very young child, Katherine was punished unmercifully whenever she exercised her imagination. At six she told a visiting Baptist clergyman that she wanted to be an actress when she grew up; at once, her viciously pious Aunt Cat flung her into the yard and administered an awful whaling.[23]

Like Katherine Anne Porter, Thomas Wolfe recalled growing up amidst recrimination and financial insecurity. The alcoholic insanity of his father, a stonecutter of Pennsylvania German extraction who had settled in Asheville, North Carolina, and the lovelessness and stinginess of his mother kept the family in a state of perpetual turmoil.[24] The Walker Percy house in a wealthy Birmingham suburb was a much quieter, gentler place, but the moodiness of LeRoy Pratt Percy sometimes wore down the naturally high spirits of the children. On one occasion, returning from his law office, the father saw his son Walker in the yard chasing his younger brother LeRoy with a rope and lightly striking at him. Infuriated beyond all rationality, the father stopped the game and forced LeRoy to hit his brother's head with the knotted end of the rope, even though he did not want to. While away at Camp Winnippee in Wisconsin in July, 1929, Walker, then thirteen, learned that his father had shot himself to death. Three years later the sixteen-year-old Walker's mother drowned, apparently without trying to rescue herself from her car which had plunged into a creek near Greenville, Mississippi.[25]

Turning from writers of fiction to poets, one finds no deviation from similar childhood circumstances of painful recollection. No poet with Southern ties had a more traumatic early history than Conrad Aiken. His father William Ford Aiken, a Harvard-trained physician in Savannah, Georgia, showed growing signs of psychotic manic-depression that led him to accuse his innocent wife Anna of all manner of infidelity and double-dealing. Dr. Aiken was so unpredictable in his outbursts, sometimes explosively aimed at the children, that his son Conrad concealed his winning a gold medal at school for fear it would bring on yet another terrorizing beating. The crazed physician was convinced his son and Anna were conspiring to put him away in an insane asylum. The climax arrived in the early morning hours of February 26, 1901. At age eleven Conrad heard two shots fired in quick succession, the sound of a body falling, and "then silence, deep and unbroken," as the Savannah *News* reported. He rushed to the master bedroom to find the slumped bodies of his parents, with a smoking .45 caliber revolver in his father's hand. With uncanny presence of mind, the child commanded the other children to stay in bed, awakened the servants in the basement rooms, ran barefoot to the nearest precinct station, and gave a coherent account of the fatalities.[26]

Needless to say, Aiken could never erase the memory of those moments and admitted that from the ravaging experience he developed a carapace to shield himself from the perils of intimacies too easily betrayed—"my trick of unexpected reticence, my impassivity of appearance, my proneness to fatigue and indifference, the rapidity with which I tire of people." In later years he translated his yearning for a mother's love and father's protective loyalty into a voracious sexual appetite, but the women he seduced were seldom objects of any genuine affection. Instead he treated them as mere "totems" of a hidden outrage. At the time of the tragedy in 1901, relatives and friends, of course, thought silence on such horrors was the best and most convenient means for wiping out memories in children. Reticence, however, drove his sense of guilt and grief deeper into himself. Yet, as in all these instances of almost numbing horrors, tragedy was translated into beauty. Aiken's "Silent Snow, Secret Snow," a short story, revealed his understanding of a child's descent into fantasy and madness.[27]

No less tragic was the case of John Gould Fletcher of Little Rock, Arkansas, one of the famous Agrarians. Born in 1886 to a wealthy New South businessman and his snobbish German wife with a long history of depression, Fletcher was reared in Lord Fauntleroy isolation in a dark mansion surrounded by an expansive lawn and high wall.[28] He had only his sister Adolphine to play with until he was sent to a local academy at age ten. Even there and later at a New England prep school he made few friends and was teased for being reclusive and physically awkward. While Fletcher was attending Harvard, his formidable and exacting father died, and the shy and irritable son, quitting college, turned to poetry to deal with his joy and guilt over what was for him a liberating event. In one poem he wrote that he could not enter the room where his father had breathed his last

> Without feeling something big and angry
> Waiting for me
> To throw me on the bed
> And press its thumbs in my throat.[29]

A difficult personality himself, Fletcher suffered a number of nervous breakdowns interspersed with periods of manic creativity. Although he won the Pulitzer Prize for poetry over William Carlos Williams in 1938, he never achieved the recognition that his sometime friend Conrad Aiken achieved, a disappointment that added to his lifelong episodes of inanition.

Like Aiken and Fletcher, Carson McCullers, though essentially a novelist, expressed her most anguished moments in verse. "Nothing resembles nothing. Yet nothing/Is not blank, It is configured Hell," she wrote in a poem that she showed to her psychiatrist. Like so many other artists, as a child she feared being unlovable and turned to her talents as the prime source of her self-confidence rather than the approval of others. The practice of art affords the chance for self-expression without the need to please others or conform to their wishes and sentiments. In her case, the greatest loss experienced as a youngster was not that of a parent but of her much adored music teacher, Mary Tucker, in Columbus, Georgia. Carson was a child prodigy at the piano. When Mary Tucker had to leave town with her husband, Carson announced at once that she was giving up music and would become a writer. Unable to express her bitterness openly, she composed stories that showed her genius but also her macabre turn of mind. Like Ellen Glasgow, she also once attempted to take her own life, and she suffered greatly from agoraphobia, a malady linked to depression.[30]

Having dealt with the record of mental distress arising from early sources of mourning, we must remember Walker Percy's suggestion that "ordeal" strengthens the soul but also stimulates the imaginative impulse as a way of coping with unpleasant, even devastating reality. "Depression," wrote the English critic Michael Ignatieff, "is a way of seeing, one which captures an essential aspect of human existence. As such, depression is both a personal catastrophe and a necessary stage in our encounter with life."[31] Certainly early and mid-twentieth-century Southern writers often met that interpretation. A drive to write that almost amounted to obsession marked each of the authors mentioned. That phenomenon was not peculiar to their careers but was almost universal in the history of western literature.

For Southern professionals, however, the fictional world they created reflected not only the personal experiences with which they wrestled but also the regional life around them. It was only natural for a Southern child to express his or her resentment of unloving or absent parents in fancies of violence and military glory that were so much a part of Southern culture. Faulkner was particularly moved as a child by the stories of Civil War valor and daring that he had heard elders recount. In the novel, *Intruder in the Dust,* he has the boy Chick Mallison relive in his imagination the famous charge of General Pickett's men and wonder how history and even his own life might have been different, had the heroic advance rolled back the Union forces. "Yesterday," Faulkner writes autobiographically, "won't be over until tomorrow and tomorrow began ten thousand years ago. For every Southern boy fourteen years old, not once but whenever he wants it, there is the instant when it's still not yet two o'clock on that July afternoon in 1863."[32]

As one of the last major writers to grow up under the regimen of an older South, Styron has identified the specialness of his homeland's literature "with a sense of tradition, of ancestry, of family, a sense of such matters as the importance of the Civil War to the history of the South, and the sense of literature as a continuous, continuing fountain."[33] "The heritage of failure and defeat—and often guilt," as literary critic Fred Hobson has observed, provided the Southern writer with "something that no other American writer, or at least American novelist, of the twentieth century had in any abundance, a tragic sense."[34] Thanks to historian Joel Williamson's study of William Faulkner, we can now also appreciate more than ever before how intertwined with a family's past were the traditional Southern problems of race relations, including sexual exploitation of black women, especially under slavery. The novelist "never openly recognized his mulatto kin," Williamson concludes, but in translating such matters into his narratives, *Absalom, Absalom!,* for instance, he was dealing with more than just a matter of abstraction, no matter how forbidden it was to voice publicly the Faulkners' intimacy with miscegenation.[35]

The second proposition asks if depression, with or without childhood origins, was peculiar to the twentieth-century Southern writer. The answer is plainly no. The difference lay in the much more repressive character of early Southern culture and the concomitant restrictions imbedded within literary fashion. In prose fiction, the moralistic adventure romance and domestic fiction dominated. The gothic form alone enjoyed currency with both readers and creators for the exploration of the interior life. The only Southern writer to surmount the limited formulae of the gothic fantasy was Edgar Allan Poe. Cruelly orphaned at an early age, Poe knew all the terrors of madness and addiction that became the subjects of his art. In 1848 he confessed to his friend George Eveleth, "I became insane, with long intervals of horrible sanity" and periods during which "I drank God only knows how long and how much." As a result, "my enemies referred the insanity to the drink rather than the drink to the insanity."[36] He once tried to commit suicide with an overdose of laudanum.[37] Lewis Simpson reads "The Fall of the House of Usher," published in 1839, as a reflection on "an enclosed plantation world— the 'garden of the chattel' I have ironically called it—and the literary mind." Simpson recognizes that Poe's Roderick Usher rules not over slaves but over "peasants," and that a sense of Southern place is never established. Actually, however, the tale concerns inheritable madness and *its* relation to the artist, a familiar topic in the gothic tradition. A political interpretation seems inappropriate: Poe belonged to the world that the preeminent mood-swinger, Lord Byron, inhabited, not to the band of do-or-die proslavery zealots. When he has Usher exclaim, "I feel that the period will sooner or later arrive when I must abandon life and reason together in some struggle with the grim phantasm FEAR," he is not concerned with armies marching southward but with a terror of death and insanity that Poe himself dreaded would soon overtake him. Nor was it merely an abstract question of a literary mind "divided against itself" in the changing values of that era. It had much more personal and, therefore, more visceral and moving a basis than literary critics assume.[38]

Unlike Poe, most Southern intellectual depressives of his era were not professional writers. The act of composing fiction for a living, particularly as the sole means of support, was deemed effeminate, particularly in the South. In the regional mind, it was merely the plaything of bored, housebound women or of female professionals like the "infamous" Harriet Beecher Stowe whose delicacy might be questioned. Admittedly, versifying, an activity with the pen that amateurs could quickly master, did furnish some degree of emotional release. Under the Byronic spell, sensitive Southerners, both men and women, found in writing soulful poems a comforting instrument. To name only three, Henry Timrod, Nathaniel Beverley Tucker, and even that Kentuckian Abraham Lincoln adopted the gloom-and-tomb formulations to ease their sense of loneliness and futility. Romantic alienation, however, had its limits even within the gothic and poetic genres; nothing could be said that defied the strict conventions about sexual impulses and other intimate matters that dwelled in the domain of sexual ambiguity and irresolution.[39]

In prose, productions that might have later become the basis for novels instead were shoved into the desk drawer, only in the last few years appearing as generally artless diaries or memoirs. Even so, the diarists, James Henry Hammond excepted, were generally very circumspect about the darker elements of life. Journal-keeping Ella Thomas of Georgia provided this insight on February 7, 1869:

> I was thoroughly out of spirits last week, dejected in body and mind. We all have our trouble, our thorn in the flesh but sometimes we are more sensitive to its piercing than others. I wonder too if there is not some truth in the remark that in every house there is a skeleton, some subject which by mutual consent it is best to avoid. I think I have a consciousness of this and when the door opens and I catch glimpses of my skeletons I try not to look but I cannot always help it, even to you my dear friend [the diary] I must not confide every thought I have.[40]

An example of a self-revealing diary, lately unearthed from dusty archives, is the embittered egotist Hammond's "secret diary," but it was scarcely introspective, having instead a self-pitying, indulgent character.[41] The modern novel form would later furnish an artistic means that both disguised and revealed. Indeed, Drew Faust's sensitive and pathbreaking *Sacred Circle*, a study of antebellum Southern intellectual life, chronicles the commiserating exchanges among Hammond, Edmund Ruffin, George Frederick Holmes, Beverley Tucker, William Gilmore Simms—several of them subject to fits of deep melancholy and to manic claims to godlike genius.[42] Nor should Hinton Rowan Helper, a North Carolina polemicist, who committed suicide late in life, be omitted. None of them, however, revealed much insight into their own lives. Rooted in the dictates of honor, shame, and duty, they externalized their inner doubts and confusions. They blamed an indifferent Southern public and Northern imperialism against their beloved slave regime for their disillusionment with the civilization around them.[43]

A single example must suffice: Edmund Ruffin, the famous Virginia advocate of agricultural reform and disunion. Ruffin much resembled in temperament many of those already discussed who lived in the following century. Like Tucker, the secessionist had lost his mother when very young; his father died when the boy was barely sixteen. A lonely, grieving child, Ruffin was reared by Thomas Cocke, a learned recluse whom he dearly loved. In 1840 Cocke, however, killed himself by placing a gun in his mouth. That event long haunted and tempted his ward until, in 1865, scrawling curses against the Yankees on a pad before pulling the trigger, Ruffin imitated Cocke's exact procedure. The old misanthrope left a body of memoirs and diaries—guileless, foreboding, but highly intriguing.[44]

The most impressive of those mildly touched by the malady, which she treated with laudanum, was Mary Chesnut, the famous South Carolina diarist. The 1883 rendition of her Civil War experiences that C. Vann Woodward edited revealed a woman frustrated. She did not have a proper genre in which to record her anguish over her barrenness, sense of irony, and shrewd insights into the ultimate futility of Confederate generals and their ladies. As Michael O'Brien recently observed, the work, with its multitude of voices, might be considered less a nostalgic reflection on the Lost Cause than a precursor of Virginia Woolf. In it, Mary Chesnut lamented, "I think this journal will be disadvantageous for me, for I spend the time now like a spider, spinning my own entrails."[45] She dared not, however, publish the work; it was too caustic and iconoclastic to suit the pieties about the war then prevailing in the South. In fact, its publication would have exiled her from respectable company, a serious matter in the still agrarian and narrow-minded post-Civil War South.

Even when a writer succeeded in overcoming the limitations of the reigning modes, the public was unprepared to approve experiments that defied current conventions. Although there were exceptions, Kate Chopin's *The Awakening* was greeted in Southern reviews with scorn and horror. So perceptive a fellow novelist as the modernist Willa Cather, a Virginian by extraction, found Chopin's greatest work trite, immodest, and inelegant. In addition, longstanding admirers misunderstood the point of her heroine Edna Pontellier's sense of futility and her suicide.[46] In other words, the approaches to art that could capture the Southern intellectual's scope of feelings simply were unavailable.

With regard to the third proposition—the importation of outside ideas—Southern writers after World War I enjoyed a lively sense of freedom in the discovery of an international literature with a modern sensibility. They were particularly attracted to those who wrote out of the same matrix of early grief and current melancholy with which the Southern intellectuals were themselves familiar. It was less the experience of serving in the Great War—few Southern literary men entered the military ranks, being, for the most part, too young—than of savoring its results—the destruction of old taboos and Edwardian primness so that even the earlier writers of fiction could be appreciated in new ways. Young William Faulkner devoured the works of the great nineteenth-century authors who had had little impact on the preceding generation of Southern writers. "I discovered," Faulkner later reminisced, "the Flauberts and Dostoyevskys and Conrads." He justly saw himself "choosing among possibilities and probabilities of behavior and weighing—and measuring each choice by the scale of the Jameses and Conrads and Balzacs."[47]

Most of the novelists Faulkner mentioned shared the melancholy sensibility. Concerning Balzac, Anthony Storr reports, throughout life the French novelist was "insatiable; hungry both for love and for fame, as if there was a void inside him which no amount of supplies outside could fill." Henry James's depressive nature is too well known to require elaboration. Gustave Flaubert, after a childhood during which, he recollected, "I dreamed of suicide," presented a cool and seemingly untroubled demeanor to the world. Even if he did not remain depressive, the author of *Madame Bovary* (1854) knew the condition well enough, and his appeal to Southern writers was strong. "His was the Word," short-story writer Peter Taylor reminisced. For many of Taylor's artistic friends during the interwar period, "he was the Master."[48]

Like Flaubert, Joseph Conrad set examples of deep introspectiveness in his somber fictional explorations of the human spirit. The Polish expatriate plunged into frequent episodes of depression, suffered a number of nervous breakdowns, and once tried to kill himself. With these experiences in mind, writing to a young aspiring novelist, Conrad advised, "You must squeeze out of yourself every sensation, every thought, every image, mercilessly . . . you must search the darkest corners of your heart."[49] (There were, of course, many other influences, most notably Marcel Proust, D. H. Lawrence, T. S. Eliot, Ezra Pound, and later Albert Camus and Jean-Paul Sartre, whose lives generally reveal similar problems with mania and depression.)[50]

Such an approach to art was the credo of Faulkner and many others who found kindred spirits in Conrad, Chekhov, Joyce, James, and other giants of literature, but most especially in Feodor Dostoyevsky. Romantic, dolorous and conservative, the Russian novelist understood both the inanition of despondency and its antidote, faith in God by which self-alienation could be overcome. In the wayfarer's search for salvation, Dostoyevsky claimed, all the negative elements of the human psyche, even a wooing of despair had to be honored as prelude to the rapture of the mystical experience.[51] Although reading his works when still too young to grasp their entire meaning, the Southern writers nevertheless sensed that Dostoyevsky spoke directly to their own artistic and temperamental needs. "The books of Dostoevski—*The Brothers Karamazov, Crime and Punishment,* and *The Idiot,*" reported Carson McCullers—"opened the door to an immense and marvelous new world." In preparing his writing career, Walker Percy was equally enthralled with the great Russian novelist and based Will Barrett of *The Last Gentleman* in part on the epileptic Prince Myshkin, Dostoyevsky's autobiographical character in *The Idiot.*[52] Charged with the new literary gospel of introspection, these mid-century writers of the South as well as their predecessors of the interwar period could leave behind provincial sanctions. Gone was the obligatory high-mindedness so long required of writers and poets of the nineteenth century. Faulkner, his generation, and their immediate successors could expose the destructiveness of the old ethic of honor even as they mourned its passing in the interwar and later Cold War worlds without moral conviction of any kind.[53]

More important, the Southern intellectuals felt free to challenge their own forebears with the powerful weapon of fiction. Thus, some of the most impressive works of Southern fiction had a common oedipal theme: Faulkner's *The Sound and the Fury* and *Absalom, Absalom!,* Allen Tate's *The Fathers,* Caroline Gordon's *Penhally,* Robert Penn Warren's *All the King's Men,* Charles Bell's *The Half-Gods,* James Agee's *Death in the Family,* Walker Percy's entire sequence of novels, Evelyn Scott's *The Narrow House,* Shelby Foote's *Tournament.* Even the traditional, hard-minded mothers of the region came under powerful fictional scrutiny. Tennessee Williams could portray his neurotic mother Edwina as Amanda Wingfield. Laurette Taylor, who played the mother in the first production of *The Glass Menag-*

erie, asked Mrs. Williams, attending the opening night, "How did you like yourself?" a question that Edwina Dakin Williams did not understand. Likewise Thomas Wolfe modeled the grasping mother of Eugene Gant on the character of his mother Julia. "Getting one's own back on parents," remarks Anthony Storr, "is a favorite pastime amongst novelists."[54]

Coupled with these parental themes was the liberating sense that now it was possible to write about dangerous interior things, particularly the unexamined complexities of human love, and even to go beyond the old, guarded euphemisms or evasions about what went on in the bedroom or in the conflicted libido. How liberating it must have seemed to fulfill Sigmund Freud's definition of a writer as one who could "perceive the hidden impulses in the minds of other people" and who could develop "the courage to let his unconscious speak."[55] Freedom to range over the psychological landscape in the manner of European fiction writers did not, however, enjoy regional celebration, a reaction that complicated most particularly the Southern writers of chronically pessimistic outlook. When Wolfe's *Look Homeward Angel* appeared in 1930, Jonathan Daniels declared that "North Carolina and the South are spat upon." Hometown folks were usually infuriated because such writers violated community reticence about whispered local scandals.[56] Living near Fort Benning, in Fayetteville, North Carolina, Carson McCullers in 1938 had the distinction of making an enemy of Mrs. George Patton, whose husband was then stationed at the military camp. The officers' wives were convinced that McCullers, "a queer duck," they agreed, had maligned them in a "weird" story published in *Harper's Bazaar.* Mrs. Patton canceled her subscription to the magazine and urged her friends to do likewise. Upon the appearance of Faulkner's *Sanctuary,* his outraged father Murry stopped a coed on the Ole Miss campus to warn that the book she was carrying "isn't fit for a nice girl to read."[57]

Censorious reaction as well as the continuing conservatism of regional life meant that in adopting the foreign importations, the Southern writer could only tread gingerly into taboo sexual territory, particularly regarding what Thomas Wolfe called "the strange first love of every boy, which is for a man."[58] The darker issues still required circumlocutions and hidden codes, but the young Faulkner experimented with a story, "Divorce in Naples," about homosexual love.[59] Even the gloomy Will Percy permitted some hints of his sexual feelings in the pages of his *Lanterns on the Levee,* published in 1941. In the customary fashion of the time, contemporaries, whether

Northern or Southern, refused to recognize Percy's allusions.[60] About September, 1941, Percy wrote his cousin John Seymour Erwin of Greenville, "In it I have, perhaps, left as much unsaid as I have said. But so much must necessarily die with us that cries out to be heard." Erwin apparently had sent him a novel, never published, that exposed forbidden themes to daylight. In reply Percy warned that such material "is just not for today. Perhaps some years hence all the inhibited will become less so and the world will develop a policy of live and let live (although I doubt this, and don't count on it.)"[61]

For those male artists who were attracted to other men, the half-liberation of the 1920s, 30s, and 40s was itself heady enough. They could read Proust and understand themes of sexual ambiguity; such inspiration may have heightened the dramatic tension of Tennessee Williams's best plays and Truman Capote's *Other Voices, Other Rooms* (1947). Yet even this well-known pair was ambivalent about sexual self-revelation. Overreacting to a few critical reviews in the midst of vast acclaim, Capote indignantly denied that his novel treated "homosexuality" at all; rather it concerned "a completely lost child" at "the moment when he gives up his boyhood."[62] With more seeming plausibility, Williams denied any relationship between his plays and his promiscuity. But just as his main characters often cannot accept or give love, so too a fear of intimacy ruled his transactions with those men and women who sacrificed themselves to meet his largely childish needs.[63]

Sexual confusion, which was more common than homosexuality, was closely related to the problem of painful but also creative depression. In stories like Henry James's "The Beast in the Jungle" (1904), Southern writers could find examples and means to express similar feelings. The life of James Agee, author of *A Death in the Family*, serves to illustrate. Like many others in this phalanx of disconsolate writers, Agee lost a parent early in life. His intoxicated father Jay died in a car crash on a lonely East Tennessee road when the worshipful child was only six. Alcoholism played general havoc in the Agee family, and James himself was not spared. Sometimes overwhelmed by his uncontrollable cycles of mania and depression, he could not work out his feelings of sexual inferiority. On one occasion, he persuaded his wife Alma and his best friend and collaborator Walker Evans to bed together while he watched with mingled emotions of desire, jealousy, and guilt. Abashed, he later tried to apologize: "However much . . . you happen to like each other, good: I am enough of an infant homosexual or postdostoevskian to be glad." But he continued in false dismissiveness, "I am enough of a 'man' not to care to think particularly whether I care or not." He tried at least once to commit suicide.[64]

Reacting to popular Southern distaste for sexual ambiguity, some Southern male writers clad themselves in the apparel of manliness and camaraderie. Certainly there were precedents: Ernest Hemingway and D. H. Lawrence, furnishing models in both their fiction and lives, encouraged such views. But the impulse for bravado had more native than foreign roots. Allen Tate was prone to challenge literary foes to duels, a familiar Southern custom, and James Branch Cabell used to brag unconvincingly of his sexual prowess in his youth. On a hunting trip in Mississippi after the announcement of winning the Nobel Prize, Faulkner's companions asked him what he would do if the Swedish ambassador were to appear and hand him the money. Standing over a basin of dirty dishes, he replied, "I'd tell him just put it on that table over there and grab a dryin' rag and help." Louis Rubin, who recounts the story, comments, "He had passed the test. He was, in other words, still one of the boys." As Rubin points out, however, the bravado had more serious uses; the artist had to keep in touch with the world he wrote about. Heavy drinking with buddies and getting off to the duck blind in a predawn chill were gratifying ways to fill that need.[65]

Finally, the fourth proposition is examined: the compulsion of the modern Southern artists to write led so often to actual or virtual suicide. Fred Hobson connects the suicidal impulse and brooding personality to the Southern writers' social alienation, fear of public reaction to their work, and sense of guilt and shame for the racial failings of the region. Although, he says, serious "South-watching" may not be "an occupational hazard," it is an intense self-identification with the region, and "an unbalanced personality" could amount to an "explosive mixture."[66] His insight adds a certain poignancy to the matter: the Southern intellectual had to bear a double burden—a conflicted relationship with his community and region *and* a deep-seated, perhaps inherited, morbidity. When at the height of their powers, this set of Southern authors often explained how much their writing was not just an occupation but a necessity, as if the work was an anchor tying them to sanity. "Being unable to write has always disturbed me as if the sky had fallen on my head," Williams wrote mournfully in his declining years.[67] "Produce again—produce; produce better than ever, and all will yet be well," Henry James once exclaimed in the depths of melancholy, a credo that the Southern writers would understand. Faulkner's drinking, which his most ardent critical admirers have generally underestimated, was very much related to his desperate need to create; both the alcoholism and the writing were means to wrestle with the demon of depression.[68] Speaking perhaps autobiographically, novelist Gail Godwin has one of her characters explain: "When she lost, even temporarily, the power to sustain an imaginative world, it was as if the real world had no meaning."[69]

For some writers the loss of former inspiration as their mental and physical deterioration grew worse led to tragic results. The difficulty was the divided mind, as these writers could not wholly free themselves from inhibitions fastened on them early in their lives. Nor could they shut out the admonishing voices of an older generation. Tennessee Williams described his highly candid memoirs as "a sort of catharsis of puritanical guilt-feelings."[70] With his rapid swings from mania to depression, Thomas Wolfe serves as a prime example of the battle between old prescriptions and new freedoms. Abusing his body with alcohol, late hours, gargantuan meals, and taxing quarrels with friends and relatives, he could not tolerate his immature dependency upon others and so struck out in every direction. At the heart of his tempestuous relationship with Aline Bernstein, a woman eighteen years older than himself, was a feeling of guilt over incest and his sense of betraying his Southern Anglo-Saxonism. He voiced his complaint in *The Web and the Rock*, when the hero shouts, "I've destroyed my youth and thrown my life away over a woman old enough to be my mother! . . . I've polluted my blood with a foul incestuous shame that all the rivers of the world could never wash away." Thus, "Jewess-haunted," as he put it, he both loved and resented his mistress who also served as his surrogate mother.[71] In 1938 his body could no longer stand the punishment; he died, age thirty-eight, from tubercule bacilli that spread rapidly from his lungs to his brain.[72]

Likewise, James Agee, who as an admiring younger writer thoroughly bored Thomas Wolfe, came to a sad end from chain-smoking, overwork, and drinking. He died in 1955 at forty-three years of age, having fatally damaged his heart. Truman Capote was another virtual suicide. Unlike Wolfe who knew very little about himself, at least Capote recognized that he was enslaved to depression and alcohol but felt helpless to do anything about the compulsions.[73]

William Faulkner, the most creative of them all, was also one of the most troubled. Frederick Karl speaks of his moody silences, which the biographer identifies as the fount of Faulkner's creativity.

We know his adoration of his mother who taught him the gift of reading, yet he seemed to resent his dependency on her out of fear of emasculation, a common enough phenomenon in the honor-conscious patriarchy of Southern life.[74] Recognizing his father's incompetence, frequent inebriation, and cold disapproval of his runty son, young Faulkner was subjected to fears of failure in life, even impotence.[75] Yet Faulkner's inner life can only be glimpsed imperfectly through the prism of his art—as he very much intended. He seldom let down his guard. Nonetheless, even as a child of twelve, he was subject to "a brooding melancholy," according to his cousin Sallie Murry. He said little about that state of mind but once recalled, "I was suddenly taken with one of those spells of loneliness and name-less sorrow that children suffer, for what or because of what they do not know." He sensed on some deep level that his mother's feelings toward him were highly ambivalent, a deprivation of love that he never overcame. Faulkner's deception of being a heroic, battle-scarred officer in the flying service in World War I suggests how far fantasy shaped his own self-image. In his later years he never admitted that he was alcoholic.[76] As Joel Williamson explains, "Bill Faulkner had grave difficulty understanding himself."[77]

Nonetheless, behind Faulkner's lengthy addiction to alcohol, which finally brought an end to serious writing, he was nursing psychic wounds that probably had genetic origins. In the Faulkner clan, as in that of so many other writers' families, alcoholism had a long history. Drinking was and still remains so much a part of Southern male custom that it would be hard to verify if the Old Colonel, the writer's great grandfather was actually an alcoholic. But certainly his grandfather, J. W. T. Faulkner, and the novelist's father Murry were both heavy inebriates who periodically went to Memphis to take the Keeley cure at a drying-out hospice. Even some of the women in the family drank enough "Prunella," the patent medicine of Victorian female choice, to give them the shakes.[78]

The connection between depression and alcoholism is so intimate that for some authors they were inseparable—with alcohol used as a sedative against depression and depression employed as an excuse for another drink. With reference to his forty-year affair with hard liquor, William Styron recently wrote, "I used alcohol as the magical conduit to fantasy and euphoria," but he came later to realize that he drank primarily "to calm the anxiety and incipient dread that I had hidden away for so long somewhere in the dungeon of my spirit."[79]

The poets of the interwar period in the South fared little better than the prose writers. John Gould Fletcher grew increasingly subject to depression as he aged. "I have a black melancholia tearing at my roots and eating like the Spartan fox at my vitals," he wrote Scott Greer.[80] Early on May 10, 1950, he left his house near Little Rock while his wife Charlie May was still asleep and walked to a nearby pond into which he plunged to end his life. Randall Jarrell, another gifted poet, versified his lament:

> I see at last that all the knowledge
> I wrung from the darkness—that the darkness flung me-
> Is worthless as ignorance: nothing comes from the nothing,
> The darkness from the darkness. Pain comes from the darkness
> And we call it wisdom. It is pain.

Making poetry of his misery, however, demonstrated that "pain" was only a part of his encounter with depression. Yet, unable to bear any more descents into mental hell, in 1964 Jarrell lunged forward in front of a passing car. Other writers during the era of the Southern Renaissance who killed themselves included the gifted journalists Clarence Cason and W. J. Cash, whose sole book-length work, *The Mind of the South*, is still considered a classic reading of the Southern ethic.[81]

Certainly this rendition of the Southern Renaissance should not be seen as a denigration of the literary achievement of the period from 1920 to 1960. First, although the stress has been upon pathology, the issue of depression by no means belittles the artistry of Faulkner and his generation. With particular reference to the melancholic and brilliant Charlotte Brontë, Sir Leslie Stephen declared over a century ago, "Great art is produced by taking an exceptionally delicate nature and mangling it slowly under the grinding wheels of the world."[82] The melancholy or the manic state begs for release in artistic expression by a process that remains mysterious but palpable. Second, many authors of that period showed few signs of mental distress. Robert Penn Warren, Allen Tate, and many others may have had their rages, quarrels, and familiarity with Jack Daniels, but they did not suffer the kind of wretchedness that Styron has phrased as a "darkness visible." Within the national literary community in which Southern writers played an almost dominant role, intellectuals such as Peter Taylor, the Tates and Warrens, and many others tried as best they could to help colleagues escape their spells of deep despair.[83] Even those afflicted tried to help each other in a writers' network of friendships. Tennessee Williams, for instance, worried much about the deteriorating health and suicidal impulses of Carson McCullers. He mused, "It might do me good to have to devote myself to someone who needed and deserved so much care." But on greater reflection he realized that "the irregularities of my life and nature—which I know I would not give up" might increase rather than assuage her "unhappiness."[84] Indeed, sometimes longstanding friendships broke irrevocably under the strain of the writers' self-generated miseries.

In summary, mania and depression provided the beleaguered writers the nutrients of creativity. As Sigmund Freud observed many years ago, artists and writers, who draw upon inner resources not open to science, "know a whole host of things between heaven and earth of which our philosophy has not yet let us dream."[85] But the same internal forces may also, in the end, tragically destroy talent and lives. What conclusions should be reached about so joyless a record? The answer may be asked in the form of a conjecture. Imagine the Southern literary resurgence *without* the writers discussed or mentioned here—Glasgow, the Percys, McCullers, Styron, Williams, Wolfe, Agee, Cash, Porter, Scott, Jarrell, Fletcher, and above all, Faulkner. For all their inner misery they not only enhanced the record of Southern letters but also largely shaped its character. They did so, however, at a cost that should proclaim them as doomed as the Confederate troops whom Faulkner's Chick Mallison dreamed about. Along with General Pickett, "with his long oiled ringlets and hat in one hand," they were waiting in the afternoon sun, as Chick Mallison imagined, until Longstreet gave "the word." That moment of cavalier glory and death appealed to the fatalistic spirit of Faulkner and his fellow writers. But when it came to artistic integrity, they had all been equally as stalwart and fearless as those Johnny Rebs at Gettysburg.[86]

Styron's Choice:

A Meditation on History, Literature, and Moral Imperatives

CHARLES JOYNER

And the people of Israel groaned under their bondage, and cried out for help, and their cry came up to God. And God heard their groaning.
—Exod. 2:23–24

The spoils taken from you will be divided among you. . . . The city will be taken, the houses plundered, the women ravished.
—Zech. 14:1–4

Then they utterly destroyed all the city, both men and women, young and old, oxen, sheep, and asses, with the edge of the sword.
—Josh. 6:21

The day dawned bleak and chill that Friday in the Virginia tidewater, and an enveloping gray light seemed to come out of the northeast. The dry leaves whispered a little in the windless November. Around noon the jailer unlocked the condemned hole of the Southampton County Jail. It was cold and musty in the hole, and the rank smell fouled the air.

For nearly two weeks Nat Turner had been lying there in darkness, secured with manacles and chains to make certain he could not escape. For nearly two weeks he had been lying there on a pine board, neither asleep nor awake, as though his very being were itself a part of darkness and silence. All he had done, all he had felt and suffered, had passed before his mind there as he had tried to explain his actions to an uncomprehending white man named Thomas Gray. It was strange to him that whites could comprehend neither motivation nor explanation for his actions. To whites he seemed to have appeared abruptly with a dark band of avenging angels to cut a red swath through Southampton County in the summer of 1831. But as Nat Turner lay upon his hard pine board in his ragged garments, he saw again how the actual and urgent need to accomplish his purpose had been revealed to him in the heavens. There had been no choice, just one right thing without alternatives, just one right thing without either falling short or overshooting. It had been as though the opposed forces of his destiny and his will had drawn swiftly together toward a foreordained mission.

Now armed guards took Nat Turner from his cell and struggled through a morass of hostile white faces. The prisoner was clothed in rags but held his head erect. The procession did not seem to progress at all but just seemed to march in place while the earth moved as they made their journey through the streets of Jerusalem, a journey that seemed to have neither definite beginning nor ending. At length the party approached a field northeast of the town. A large crowd, sullenly inert and immobile, had gathered around a gnarled old live oak.

The sheriff asked the prisoner if he had anything to say. Turning slowly, quietly, holding his body erect, Nat Turner answered in an unexpectedly pleasant voice. "I'm ready" was all he said. Then, waiting under the tree without impatience or even emotion, he stared out beyond the mob of hostile white faces into the distant skies. They threw one end of the rope over a limb of the tree and pulled him up with a jerk. Eyewitnesses said Nat Turner did not move a muscle; he hung there as still as a rock.

So they hanged Nat Turner from a live oak tree in 1831. They skinned his body and rendered his flesh into grease. They sliced a souvenir purse from his skin and divided his bones into trophies, to be handed down as family heirlooms.[1] If all this was supposed to have killed Nat Turner, it would seem to have failed miserably. Nat Turner still lives in history, for he led the greatest slave revolt ever to take place in the greatest slave republic in the New World. No one has yet been able to explain satisfactorily the tragic enigma of Nat Turner, the spiritual and charismatic young carpenter with visions of apocalypse who at the age of thirty-one was taken to Jerusalem to hang upon a tree.[2]

William Styron left his native Virginia in the 1940s, but in his novel, *The Confessions of Nat Turner*, he goes home again. "It took place not far from where I was born," he told his friend James Jones as early as 1963, adding that the idea of writing a book on the rebellion was "something that I've been thinking about for fifteen years." He believed that the Nat Turner rebellion was "the most important thing that happened in the history of Southampton County." He eventually decided to write the book in the early 1960s. "As with everything I've ever written, I took long recesses from it. Several times I was baffled by the way the book was going. Once, I abandoned it for six or seven months. But then I knuckled down and the structure came as I wrote." His *Confessions of Nat Turner* "wasn't something that I conceived in some great Jovian way in the beginning."[3]

The form of Styron's *Confessions* is pervaded by frames, by memories of memories, by stories within stories, centering his protagonist within a novel that brings him out of the opaque darkness of the past through his contact with a white lawyer named Thomas Gray.[4] Part 1 opens with the rebel caged, awaiting his trial and telling his story of the uprising to lawyer Gray. "I knew with this book that the place I had to start was with Nat in his cell," Styron told an interviewer. "Since the last scene had to do with his death, the first one had to partake of that, too."[5] In this section Styron explores the enigma of Nat Turner in his conversations with Gray, in his selective recollections as he tries to come to terms with his memories, in his snatches of conversation whispered through the jail wall to a fellow conspirator, and in the trial itself. In Styron's *Confessions* Nat is as fascinated by the paradox of Thomas Gray as Gray is by the riddle of Nat Turner. Nat has "an impression, dim and fleeting, of hallucination, of talk buried deep in dreams." He stares at this strange white man, concluding that he is "little different from any of the others." Still he found it "a matter of wonder" where "this my last white man (save the one with the rope) had come from." He sometimes felt that he had "made him up." Since it was hard "to talk to an invention," Nat Turner resolved to remain "all the more determinedly silent."[6]

The core of Styron's *Confessions* is the story of Nat's early life, portrayed in a flashback constituting most of the novel, framed by his execution. It takes the form of a pastiche of the slave narrative genre. "My mother's mother was a girl of the Coromantee tribe from the

Gold Coast," Styron's Nat reports, "thirteen years old when she was brought in chains to Yorktown aboard a schooner sailing out of Newport, Rhode Island, and only a few months older when she was sold at auction beneath a huge live oak tree in the harborside town of Hampton, to Alpheus Turner." She died in childbirth the same year, survived only by Nat's mother.[7]

If Styron's Nat is born in bondage and remains conscious of his invisible chains, he is nevertheless spoiled by benevolent paternalism. As the son of a scullery maid and cook, he grows up in the Big House, scornful of the field hands he considers to be "creatures beneath contempt." If a "wretched cornfield hand, sweating and stinking," approached the front veranda of the Big House in need of medical assistance after gashing his bare foot with a hoe," Styron has his fictional Nat Turner recall, "I would direct him to the proper rear door in a voice edged with icy scorn." To Styron's Nat, the mass of the plantation slaves were "so devoid of the attributes I had come to connect with the sheltered and respectable life that they were not even worth my derision."[8]

Styron's Nat, his disdain for blackness balanced by a reverence for whiteness, dreams of being white. Waiting on a deserted plantation, he fantasizes about possessing the plantation: "In a twinkling I became white—white as clabber cheese, white, stark white, white as a Marble Episcopalian. . . . Now, looking down at the shops and barns and cabins and distant fields, I was no longer the grinning black boy in velvet pantaloons, for a fleeting moment instead I owned all, and so exercised the privilege of ownership by unlacing my fly and pissing loudly on the same worn stone where dainty tiptoeing feet had gained the veranda steps a short three years before. What a strange, demented ecstasy! How white I was! What wicked joy!"[9]

Styron's young slave is greatly affected by a "good master," Samuel Turner, whose surname he assumes and who introduces him to the idea of hope. When Nat steals a book, his master sees proof that slaves are, after all, "capable of intellectual enlightenment and enrichment of the spirit." So he and his wife begin an educational experiment, giving Nat a Bible and teaching him to read. The brilliant young pupil memorizes many scriptural passages and comes to know the Bible better than some of the local white preachers. Aware of his own charm and intelligence, aware that he has been spared the harshness and brutality that most slaves have to endure, Styron's Nat grows accustomed to affection from everyone. "I became in short a pet," he says, "the darling, the little black jewel of Turner's Mill. Pampered, fondled, nudged, pinched, I was the household's spoiled child." The young slave feels a regard toward his master, Samuel Turner, "very close to the feeling one should bear only toward the Divinity." Between them are not only "strong ties of emotion," but "a kind of love."[10]

Samuel Turner gives his precocious young slave training, encouragement, and responsibilities. Eventually, three years before Nat comes of age, Samuel Turner promises to set him free. The young slave is initially appalled by the prospect. After all, servitude and a kindly master are all that he has known. He wonders what would have become of him if his life had continued without the promise of freedom. His meditation is an eloquent account of what "slavery at its best" might mean. Without the hope of freedom, he might have become "an ordinary, run-of-the-mill house nigger, mildly efficient at some stupid task like wringing chickens' necks or smoking hams or polishing silver." He probably would have become "a malingerer whenever possible," although he would have been "too jealous of my security to risk real censure or trouble," would have been "cautious in my tiny thefts, circumspect in the secrecy of my afternoon naps, furtive in my anxious lecheries with the plump yellow-skinned cleaning maids upstairs in the dark attic." He muses that he probably would have grown "ever more servile and unctuous as I became older," would have become a "crafty flatterer on the lookout for some bonus of flannel or stew beef or tobacco," all the while developing "a kind of purse-lipped dignity" behind his "stately paunch and fancy bib and waistcoat." He would have become a "well loved" and "palsied stroker of the silken pates of little white grandchildren," although "rheumatic, illiterate, and filled with sleepiness, half yearning for that lonely death which at long last would lead me to rest in some tumbledown graveyard tangled with chokeberry and jimson weed." He would be known, of course, as Uncle Nat. As things turn out, Nat becomes instead a carpenter, a skilled craftsman, an asset to his white masters. At the same time he becomes a preacher to his own people. Yet the foretaste of freedom only excites growing hunger. His life takes on new direction. In one morning, in one glimpse of the possibilities of the future, Samuel Turner converts his little slave Nat into a human being burning to be free.[11]

Then the tidewater land goes sterile and Samuel Turner goes bankrupt. Forced to sell out and move to Alabama, he abandons his plan to free his pet slave. At the age of twenty, Styron's Nat is on the threshold of freedom when he suddenly realizes that slavery is "the *true* world in which a Negro moves and breathes." To learn that even his beloved Marse Samuel could treat slaves so inhumanly is "like being plunged into freezing water." Samuel Turner hands Nat over to a fanatical Baptist minister, the epitome of ecclesiastical evil. Although the preacher is legally obliged to free the young slave in a stated time, Nat gets a year's taste of just how bad slavery can be before he is sold for $460. He is then forced to submit to a succession of stupid, brutal, and swinish slaveholders. They beat him and half-starve him. They subject him to every kind of humiliation. For Styron's Nat, the dream of freedom is shattered; he knows that the slaveholders are his moral inferiors.[12]

From such experiences Styron's Nat learns "how greatly various were the moral attributes of white men who possessed slaves, how different each owner might be by way of severity or benevolence." Slaveholders range "from the saintly (Samuel Turner) to the all right (Moore) to the barely tolerable (Reverend Eppes) to a few who were unconditionally monstrous." But "the more tolerable and human white people became in their dealings with me," Styron's Nat observes, "the keener was my passion to destroy them." Nat Turner's revolt is not represented in the novel as the irrepressible rage of the intolerably oppressed. Instead, Styron's Nat directs his deepest anger against Samuel Turner, the man who first held out to him the prospect of freedom.[13]

Turning more and more to the Bible for consolation, Nat Turner recognizes the bitter truth of Ecclesiastes: "The preacher was right. He that increaseth knowledge increaseth sorrow." He nourishes his newfound hatred of whites on the harsh words of the prophets, on the promise of vengeance to be visited upon the enemies of righteousness, upon the enemies of God's chosen people.[14]

Nat's years with one cruel master last nearly a decade and seem twice as long. Thomas Moore "hated all Negroes with a blind, obsessive hatred which verged upon a kind of minor daily ecstasy." For nearly a decade Nat feeds on Old Testament prophets and nurtures a hatred so bitter it verges on madness. Styron's Nat is strictly an Old Testament figure; he thinks and speaks in the blood-stained rhetoric of his Hebrew heroes Ezekiel, Daniel, Isaiah, and Jeremiah. For nearly a decade scriptural poetry weaves in and out of his ruminations. He fasts and prays in the wilderness and waits for a sign that eventually comes: in the "midst of the rent in the clouds" he sees "a black angel clothed in black armor with black wings outspread from east to west; gigantic, hovering, he spoke in a thunderous voice louder than anything I had ever heard: 'Fear God and give glory to Him for the hour of His judgment is come.'" After such visions Nat has little doubt of his mission. And the sins of the white fathers visited upon their black slaves leave him little doubt of his method. With great care and with great intelligence he begins to plan his strategy of extermination.[15]

For nearly a decade Nat's camouflage is to become "a paragon of rectitude, of alacrity, of lively industriousness, of sweet equanimity and uncomplaining obedience." He becomes a keen observer of slave personality types, not only of those given to "wallowing in the dust at the slightest provocation, midriffs clutched in idiot laughter," those who "endear themselves to all, white and black, through droll interminable tales about ha'nts and witches and conjures," but also of those who "reverse this procedure entirely and in *their* niggerness are able to outdo many white people in presenting to the world a grotesque swagger," a posture suited to the black driver or the tyrannical kitchen mammy and butler, who were skilled in keeping "safely this side of insolence."[16]

Styron's Nat chooses to cast himself in the role of a promising young slave given to "humility, a soft voice, and houndlike obedience." He learns how to affect that "respect and deference it is wise for any Negro to assume" in the presence of a strange white man. He learns to shuffle and scrape and to adopt obsequious field hand accents and postures. He learns how to "merge faceless and nameless with the common swarm," how "to interpret the *tone* of what is being said," and how to sense danger. But Styron's Nat Turner is always conscious of "the weird unnaturalness of this adopted role," always counseling himself "to patience, patience, *patience* to the end," always biding his time.[17]

But the wait is not aimless; Nat spends much of it enlisting potential recruits for his divine mission of vengeance and liberation. He often loses heart as he observes his fellow slaves "half drowned from birth in a kind of murky mindlessness," their mouths agape in "sloppy uncomprehending smiles, shuffling their feet." They seem to him "as meaningless and as stupid as a barnful of mules," and he "hate[s] them one and all." But he also feels "a kind of wild, desperate love for them." He is ambivalent toward Hark, whom he hopes to make one of his commanders. Hark, he muses, has "the face of an African chieftain," a godlike frame and strength, and a mortal grievance against his master for selling his wife and child. "Yet the very sight of white skin cowed him, humbled him to the most servile abasement." Nat is enraged by Hark's "dull, malleable docility." When in the presence of any white, Hark unconsciously becomes "the unspeakable bootlicking Sambo, all giggles and smirks and oily, sniveling, servility." Hark's only excuse is that he is overwhelmed by "dat black-assed feelin'." The expression, Nat concedes, perfectly expresses what he calls "the numbness and dread which dwells in every Negro's heart."[18]

Styron's narrative flows relentlessly toward Nat's appointment with apocalypse. Preparing for the hour of the bloodbath, Nat seeks out those slaves "in whom hatred was already ablaze" and cultivates "hatred in the few remaining and vulnerable." He tests and probes, "warily discarding those in whom pure hatred could not be nurtured and whom therefore I could not trust." Tirelessly he strains to instill in his followers confidence in themselves and faith in their leader. Tirelessly he strains to overcome their fears. After all, he asks, what have slaves to lose but their chains?[19]

When the time comes for their long march through the Virginia countryside, Nat's rebels hack off heads as if their aim were vengeance rather than freedom. In the predawn darkness of August 22, 1831, they wander from house to house severing limbs, crushing skulls, and slaughtering every white man, woman, and child in their path. But when Nat raises his axe over his master's head, his hand shakes so much his blow misses. Over and over, between violent seizures of vomiting, Nat tries to kill. Over and over he fails. Among the scores slain by the rebels, Nat takes but one life: that of the sympathetic young girl Margaret Whitehead, "her dimpled chin tilted up as . . . she carols heavenward, a radiance like daybreak on her serene young face," the one white person he still loves, the one white person whose "closeness stifled me . . . wafting toward me her odor—a disturbing smell of young-girl sweat mingled with the faint sting of lavender."[20]

Once the slaughter of the whites is over, the slaughter of the blacks begins. Virginia's defense of slavery is even bloodier than Nat Turner's revolt against it. Nat and his black followers are hunted down, tried, and executed. They have killed sixty whites. White Virginians in reprisal kill more than two hundred blacks, only a few of them involved in the rebellion at all. At Nat's trial, Thomas Gray tells the court that "save in the inexplicably successful murder of Margaret Whitehead—inexplicably motivated, likewise obscurely executed—the defendant, this purported bold, intrepid, and resourceful leader, was unable to carry out *a single feat of arms!* Not only this, but at the end his quality of leadership, such as it was, utterly deserted him!" He tells the court that "pure Negro cowardice" explains "this base crime—the slaying not of a virile and stalwart man but of a fragile, weak, and helpless young maiden but a few years out of childhood." He tells the court that "all such rebellions are not only exceedingly rare in occurrence but are ultimately doomed to failure, and this as a result of the basic weakness and inferiority, the moral deficiency of the Negro's character.[21]

Awaiting his execution, Styron's Nat has an erotic fantasy about Margaret Whitehead, a kind of symbolic sacrament of extreme unction. "And as I think of her, the desire swells within me and I am stirred by a longing so great," he muses, "it seems more than my heart can abide. *Beloved, let us love one another: for love is of God; and everyone that loveth is born of God, and knoweth God.*" In the darkness of his cell, "I feel the warmth flow into my loins and my legs tingle with desire. I tremble and I search for her face in my mind, seek her young body, yearning for her suddenly with a rage that racks me with a craving beyond pain; with tender stroking motions I pour out my love within her; pulsing flood; she arches against me, cries out, and the twain—black and white—are one."[22] As he is led to his execution, Styron's Nat reflects, "I would have done it all again. I would have destroyed them all. Yet I would have spared one. I would have spared her that showed me Him whose presence I had not fathomed or maybe never even known."[23]

But Nat Turner would not die. He set the House of Bondage on fire. He made history, and he lives in history. "I think this may be a valuable book in a certain way," Styron told an interviewer in 1967. "Very few people know anything about slavery and Negro history, and I don't know of any modern work of fiction that has touched on the problem. Writers probably have been intimidated by the sheer, awesome fact of what it must have been to be a slave. I just had to seize the bull by the horns and become one."[24]

The boldest choice William Styron made was to "become one," to assume the persona of Nat Turner. White authors, whether looking up an avenue of live oaks leading to a plantation Big House or up a red clay road leading to a sharecropper's shack, had customarily viewed the South through the eyes of white Southerners. Preoccupied with the moral problems of white people and guilt-stricken at white brutality toward blacks, modern white writers had often been guided by impulses of contrition and expiation. And modern black critics had often come to take for granted such contrition and expiation on the part of guilt-stricken white writers. But in *The Confessions of*

Nat Turner Styron chose as his point of view to look through a black lens, chose to try to see Nat's world from behind the black mask. His decision to write the book in the first person, to let Nat tell his own story, was a crucial decision.

With no participants leaving behind firsthand accounts and no white victims living to tell the tale, evidence is inevitably scanty. Styron felt he had little to go on beyond his own imagination. The best-known source is a twenty-page pamphlet, "The Confessions of Nat Turner," written by Thomas Gray, a Virginia lawyer who interviewed Turner in the Southampton County jail. Beyond that, Styron "invented almost everything except what was directly connected with the revolt."[25]

Before 1968 William Styron was relatively obscure, at least to the general public; thereafter he was notorious. His *Confessions* became for a time the moral storm center of American history. Perhaps it could not have been otherwise. As C. Vann Woodward observes, "Slavery was, after all, the basic moral paradox of American history." Styron's novel was not without honor. It won the Pulitzer Prize for fiction and indelibly inscribed his representation of Nat Turner on America's consciousness.[26] But Styron's *Confessions* also stimulated alarmed reactions and infuriated complaints in some quarters. The novel was widely condemned for all sorts of sins, and his critics were not reluctant to be blunt. Some of the scandalized permitted their reviews to degenerate into polemic. Nat Turner lives in history, they argued, but not in the pages of Styron's novel.[27]

If Styron found the initial responses dismaying, worse was to come. A group of black intellectuals who, as Albert Murray put it, took it upon themselves to "keep check on such things," wrote a book-length response under the collective sobriquet "Ten Black Writers." Their objections were primarily that, beneath a facade of Southern liberalism, Styron's *Confessions* paraded such racist stereotypes as black cowardice, incompetence, and immorality; the decline of black family values; and black sexual preoccupation with white women. Styron, they charged, had corrupted the historical record by inadequate research and misuse of documents and had constructed a novel entirely lacking in historical substance and literary merit (his Pulitzer Prize notwithstanding).[28]

The Ten did not find credible what they called the "vacillating introspection" of Styron's protagonist. He was a Nat Turner that whites could accept, they said, but he was emphatically not the Nat of "the living traditions of black America." He was not the "hero with whom Negroes identify." According to them, the real Nat Turner was "a virile, commanding, courageous figure" who "killed or ordered killed real white people for real historical reasons." They faulted Styron for his abhorrent attribution of ambivalence, complexity, and mixed motives to the man they called "our black rebel." Styron's *Confessions*, they charged, were "part of the whitened appropriation of our history by those who have neither eaten nor mourned." The novelist, "unable to eat and digest the blackness, the fierce religious conviction, the power of the man," had substituted "an impotent, cowardly, irresolute creature of his own imagination." Styron's Nat, they complained, is not powerful but pathetic, not Othello but Hamlet, not a folk hero but a groveling, grinning Uncle Tom, prancing about the piazza while kindly ole Cunnel Massa benevolently sips his julep. To be sure, Styron's Nat is only intermittently groveling (and deceptively so, at that); but he is hardly the single-minded black nationalist revolutionary constructed by the Ten Black Writers.[29]

Nor was their attitude toward what they called "Styron's assault on Nat Turner's family" any more favorable. The Ten contrasted the female-headed family of Styron's Nat with that of the historical Nat Turner. Growing up in a "strong family unit," they said, "buttressed his sense of identity and mission." They pointed out that the historical Nat told Thomas Gray his early religious inspiration and teaching came from his parents and his grandmother. Styron, however, minimizes their influence. In his hands Nat's main religious influence comes from a white family, especially from the young daughters of the family. The Ten charged that Styron's change wrenches Nat Turner out of the unique context of African-American religion.[30]

Styron, the Ten contended, devalues the historical presence and influence of the black family. They pointed out that in Gray's *Confessions*, Turner fondly recalled his beloved grandmother whom he describes as "very religious, and to whom I was much attached." Styron's Nat, however, tells Gray that "I never laid eyes on my grandmother." She "is immediately banished" from Styron's book. Also in Gray's *Confessions* Nat remembered his father and mother, who had taught him to read and write, with special fondness. When he was three or four, he recalled, he was told that "I surely would be a prophet, as the Lord had shewn me things that had happened before my birth. And my father and mother strengthened me in this my first impression, saying in my presence, I was intended for some great purpose, which they had always thought from certain marks on my breast." In his *Confessions*, Styron alters the line to read, "And my mother strengthened me in this my first impression. . . ." It is not surprising that, to the Ten, that appeared "a remarkably revealing translation"; the white Virginian had not only eliminated the African grandmother, but also the troublesome father.[31]

The Ten were vexed by Styron's "psychoanalytical emphasis upon Nat's so-called tormented relationship with his father following psychoanalyst Erik Erikson's book *Young Man Luther.*" The historical Nat Turner, they noted, had told Thomas Gray that he had become convinced by "my father and mother" that he was "intended for some great purpose." The Ten believed Nat's discontent with slavery may very well have been inspired by his father, who had escaped from the plantation. Nat himself escaped when placed under a new overseer, but he returned to the plantation after a month out in the woods. His fellow slaves, dismayed at his return, told him that if they had his intelligence, "they would not serve any master in the world."[32]

Styron's representation of Nat Turner as a house slave also troubled the Ten. They complained that Styron "detaches mother and son from black people" by making his mother a "house nigger," when "according to tradition" (unspecified) she was an African who hated slavery so much she had to be tied at Nat's birth to keep her from murdering him. By giving his fictional Nat a white upbringing and white values, by separating him from the slave community and making him contemptuous of his fellow blacks, they claimed, Styron reduces the significance of the historical insurrection to little more than fear and self-loathing in Tidewater Virginia. The insurrection of the historical Nat Turner, they insisted, was driven by love, not hatred, for his fellow slaves.[33]

What the Ten called "the apologist theme" running through Styron's *Confessions* came in for special condemnation. Styron, the grandson of slaveholders, portrays a gallery of his ancestors ranging across a spectrum from "saintly" to "all right" to "barely tolerable" to "monstrous." In their opinion "a master was a master was a master." Styron fails, they declared, to portray "American slavery as the cruelest, most inhuman, slavery system in the entire recorded history of man's bestiality to man." They found the obvious explanation for his "failure" to see what was so clear to them in Styron's "preconceptions of black inferiority." They did not attempt to explain the paradox of a cruel and dehumanizing system that failed to dehumanize its victims.[34]

The most conspicuous complaints clustered around Styron's representation of Nat Turner as a celibate who sublimates his sexual drives into fantasies and into a religious fanaticism that inspires his revolt. The homosexual and asexual tendencies Styron invents for Nat proved especially controversial. The Ten accused him of denying Nat Turner's manhood. According to them Styron roots Nat's apocalyptic religious vision in sexual perversion, downplaying his religious fervor. The closest Styron's version of Nat Turner comes to a realized sexual experience is homosexual experiments with another young black slave, from which he comes to his baptism burdened with guilt. According to them it was an attack on the manhood of "our black rebel," implying that he was "not a man at all" and suggesting Nat was "really feminine." According to them there was nothing in the historical record to suggest that "Nat had no love whatever for black women, which is how Styron depicts him. As a matter of fact, he was married to one, but you wouldn't know it from the novel." Nor is there anything to suggest "Nat's great lust and passion for white women, but this is the way he is presented throughout Styron's novel." According to them Styron ignores evidence that the historical Nat Turner had a black wife in order to fabricate an ambivalent (and wholly fictional) romance between Nat and Margaret Whitehead, a white girl whom Styron's Nat loves and toward whom he deflects his sexual drives platonically. But she is also the only white person he kills with his own hands during the uprising. According to them this relationship exemplifies the racist stereotype of black men lusting after white women. Clearly, they believed, "Styron feels that Nat Turner's emotional attachment to this white 'forbidden fruit' was a key factor in his psychological motivation." The Ten found Styron's book tainted by his talent as a novelist. The artist had used his art "to reconcile Nat Turner to an unacceptable reality by making him confess that he would have spared at least one white person. ("Go ye into the city and find one . . . just one.") Thus, they said, "the child-woman, Margaret, who was a victim of history, becomes the central image by which Styron rejects history." The interracial love affair with Margaret had nothing to do with Nat Turner and the slave experience, they maintained. It had everything to do with Styron's own fantasies and Styron's own racism.[35]

Nor did the Ten find other black men in the novel faring any better at Styron's hands. They were particularly infuriated at his portrait of Will—the slave rebel who kills more voraciously than any other—as "a lunatic hell-bent on raping white women." In what they call "Styron's fantasy," Will joins the revolution because he wants to "get me some of dat white stuff." The fictional Nat Turner is put off by the "foaming and frenzied nature of his madness," but the Ten absolved the historical Will of any guilt during the insurrection except that of "dispatching" a number of whites with a single-minded efficiency. Their verdict is that "like Joshua, he is simply engaged in the destruction of the Lord's enemies." In the novel Nat warns his followers, "Do not unto their women what they have done to thine." Despite his injunction, however, soon "this scarred, tortured little black man was consummating at last ten thousand old swollen moments of frantic and unappeasable desire" between "Miss Sarah's thrashing, naked thighs." Styron's purpose appeared transparent to the Ten. "It looks," they proclaimed, "as if nigger-beast has struck again." Could a black man be motivated to such a large-scale assault on white lives, they asked rhetorically, only by sex and insanity?[36]

"Styron's fantasy," the Ten declared, attempts to undercut the black rebel's "credentials as a leader" by presenting him as "a panicky, fearful, impotent man," unable to strike a death blow. They saw Nat Turner as a heroic military commander, who "initiated the rebellion by striking his master with a hatchet." In the dark the hatchet glanced from his master's head and Nat was unable to kill him. Will "laid him dead." "General Nat," as they explained it, was "the *leader* of the Southampton insurrection, and generals seldom kill." They pointed out that General Nat sent "fifteen or twenty of the best armed and most to be relied on" to approach the houses as fast as their horses could run." This was intended to strike terror among the inhabitants and prevent them from escaping. As a result he "never got to the houses" until after "the murders were committed," although he occasionally arrived in time to see "the work of death completed, viewed the mangled bodies as they lay, in silent satisfaction, and immediately started in quest of other victims."[37]

The Ten also objected to Styron's portraying Nat Turner after the murders as "remorseful" and "contrite," as "alone and forsaken," and as feeling "a terrible emptiness." Styron, they claimed, "has coerced poor Nat Turner into a full confession, proving—beyond a shadow of doubt—the vengeful ingratitude of a literate, pampered slave for his benevolent masters, an ingratitude which turns unprovoked into hatred and murder!" Nat Turner, they insisted, was calm and cool to the end.[38]

Nat Turner's insurrection, as the Ten Black Writers saw it, had yet to be fully appreciated and understood. It was the most profound historical experience of African Americans. What was needed (and what Styron did not supply) was attention to an African American oral tradition of Nat Turner as an "epic hero, a special, dedicated breed of man who had given his last full measure of devotion to liberation and dignity." The tradition asserted by the Ten is very much at odds with Styron's fictional creation. His Nat Turner "is one whom many white people will accept at a safe distance," but he "is not the hero with whom Negroes identify." Styron's protagonist, they noted with irritation, is "a Nat Turner who is simply not to be found in the astringent report of Lawyer Gray, or in the living traditions of black America."[39]

"The voice in this confession," the Ten charged, is not the voice of Nat Turner but "the voice of William Styron." And the images are not the images of Nat Turner but "the images of William Styron. The confession is the confession of William Styron." According to them the fictional Nat Turner embodies "a lot of Styron's own personality." According to them his "selection of 'factual' and psychological material speaks for itself."[40]

Styron was stung by the criticisms of the Ten. Confronted with the furious reception of his *Confessions,* already dubious about critics, shy and uncomfortable as a public speaker, he was rarely very effective in his own defense. I was present in 1968 at a discussion of fiction and history among Styron, Robert Penn Warren, Ralph Ellison, and C. Vann Woodward. Eugene Genovese had organized the panel for the annual meeting of the Southern Historical Association. There Ellison defended Styron against the charges of racism and bigotry, and Woodward defended him against the charges that he had falsified history. But one of the Ten relentlessly taunted Styron from the audience: "I can remember that the last time I called you a liar, it became very bitter," he heckled. "It seems as though we confront each other from the North to the South. I met you in Massachusetts this summer, and now all the way down in New Orleans I'm here to call you a liar again." Inexperienced in such skilled polemics, Styron fell into his antagonist's trap, responding irritably that "indeed you have haunted me. You're my *bête noir.*"[41]

At times Styron insisted ineptly on his fidelity to the evidence, despite considerable evidence to the contrary. At other times he responded to charges that he ignored historical scholarship by demanding "When were writers of historical novels obligated in any way to acknowledge the work of historians?" On such occasions he claimed impatiently that it is the "right and privilege" of the novelist "to substitute imagination for facts," that "if perfect accuracy had been my aim, I would have written a work of history rather than a

novel." On another occasion he told an interviewer that "an obsession with absolute accuracy is impossible if you are writing a novel
dealing with history. It becomes ridiculous, simply because you are
writing a novel." Such a defense might have been more impressive
had he not explicitly denied in his author's note to *The Confessions
of Nat Turner* that it was a historical novel (a genre he considered
"disreputable"). He called his book rather a "meditation on history"
and boasted that he had not made up anything that ran counter to
the evidence. "I have rarely departed from the *known* facts about Nat
Turner and the revolt of which he was the leader," he wrote, and he
said he had allowed himself to use "freedom of imagination in reconstructing events" only "in those areas where there is little knowledge
in regard to Nat."[42]

Precisely what Styron meant by the term "meditation on history" is unclear. In a 1968 interview he conceded that "I've found
that the phrase 'meditation on history' has buffaloed quite a few
people, and I've never really been able to figure out just what I meant
by it." If a "meditation on history" would be expected to bear a greater
resemblance to historical reality than would an historical novel,
Styron would seem to have flunked badly. In fact, he seems to have
assumed that a "meditation on history" required lesser, rather than a
greater, obligation of fidelity to the historical record. What he considered "known facts," for example, seems to have meant facts known
to *him*; and "areas where there is little knowledge" seems to have
referred merely to areas in which *he* had little knowledge. As he was
writing the book, he bragged to interviewers of his having mastered
the sources. The evidence consisted of Gray's *Confessions,* "a few little newspaper clippings of the time, all of them seemingly sort of
halfway informed and hysterical and probably not very reliable," and
a "biased book" published "seventy years after the event" by "a very
proslavery" Virginia historian, one William S. Drewry. "Basically," he
said, "these few are the only documents on the insurrection." It is
true that evidence regarding Nat Turner is relatively scanty, but it is
not quite so scanty as Styron assumed. It is true that the evidence
is incomplete, but incomplete as it is, there is sufficient surviving
historical evidence to suggest a rather different Nat Turner from the
one depicted in his pages. Styron sought the historian's authority
without the historian's discipline. As historian Bertram Wyatt-Brown
put it, he "showed contempt for what historians must always demand—an attentiveness to accuracy and substantiation."[43]

Back and forth the controversy went, occasionally in civilized low key, more often at shrill pitch, depending on the temperaments of attackers and defenders. The most vigorous defense came not from the author himself, but from historian Eugene D. Genovese, who responded to the attacks with ample polemical skills of his own.[44] The Ten had insisted that "the historical data reveal the real Nat as commanding, virile, and courageous." Genovese retorted, "The historical data reveal no such thing. In fact, they do not reveal much at all about Nat Turner's qualities." Nor did Styron acknowledge that "the historical data" revealed any such virility, courage, and commanding qualities. "The facts tell us this," he said, "that if you examine the testimony, the original *Confessions*, any intelligent person is going to be appalled by this vision of a heroic figure, because he's not very heroic looking at all. He looks like a *nut* who gathers together several followers, plows through a county one evening, admittedly without even having devised a plan, and kills fifty-some white people, most of whom are helpless children. *Big Deal!* Fine hero." If Nat Turner's revolt was unable to kill the domestic institution, it killed something more vulnerable than its white victims. As historian William Freehling has observed, Turner's rebels murdered the "slaveholders' domestic illusions," and white Virginians "turned the Domestic Institution into an anti-domestic prison." The Virginia debate over slavery the following year resulted not in emancipation but in slavery being clamped even more tightly on the Old Dominion. The insurrection had resulted in catastrophe, not only for Nat Turner and of course for the white victims, but especially for the slaves. Genovese denied that Styron convicted Nat Turner of cowardice. "The inner conflict and pain can be interpreted as cowardice and irresolution by those who wish to do so," he wrote, "but this interpretation seems to me more revealing of its authors than of either Styron or the historical Turner." On the other hand, Genovese pronounced Gray's *Confessions* suspect. Gray was a disinherited and downwardly mobile white slaveholder who was hardly free of the passions stirred up by the rebellion. Turner's testimony to Gray was ambiguous evidence that could be read as "the reflections of one of those religious fanatics whose single-minded madness carried him to the leadership of a popular cause." Of course Nat Turner tried to make himself appear to Gray "as if he always knew what he was doing," Genovese noted, but under the circumstances could his testimony really be taken for anything more than the words of a man with "no wish to bare his innermost thoughts to the enemy?"[45]

Styron's critics had maintained that, far from being contemptuous of his fellow slaves, the historical Nat Turner was driven by love, not hatred, for his people. But Genovese insisted that Styron's Nat *had* expressed such love in the novel. Had he not loved his people, he "would not have protested so much against their weakness in the face of oppression; he could not even have perceived them as victims of oppression." His condemnation of them, Genovese believed, was "essentially a hatred for the oppression rather than for the oppressed." It was the kind hatred from which no revolutionary could ever be entirely free. Not even the fiery orator David Walker, whose "magnificent call for slave insurrection" in 1829 may have inspired Nat Turner's action, ever "feared to mix the professions of love for his people with the harshest condemnation," according to Genovese. "Why is it," Walker demanded, "that those few, weak, good for nothing whites are able to keep so many able men, one of whom can put to flight a dozen whites, in wretchedness and misery?" It was, he said, because blacks were "ignorant, abject, servile, and mean—and the whites know it, they know that we are too servile to assert our rights as men—or they would not fool with us as they do." And "why do they not bring the inhabitants of Asia to be body servants to them?" he asked. "They know they would get their bodies rent and torn asunder from head to foot." That humanity, Genovese declared, the humanity of such a genuine revolutionary as David Walker, the "humanity of men capable of doubt and anguish," was what Styron gave to his Nat Turner.[46]

The Ten faulted Styron for ignoring Walker's *Appeal*, insisting that Nat must have "read and been inspired, yes inflamed" by the pamphlet they regarded as "the most inflammatory indictment of slavery ever written." For them, the question was why Styron did not motivate Nat Turner with Walker's *Appeal*. "Was he unaware of it?" they asked. "Or was he trying to give the impression that there was little evidence of unrest amongst the black folk? And that Nat Turner was some kind of freak among his brethren?" Certainly at the time Virginia's Governor John Floyd, was "fully convinced" that Walker's "incendiary" pamphlet had been read from the pulpits by "every black preacher, in the whole country east of the Blue Ridge."[47]

It is true that many of the slaves in Styron's novel personify the kind of stereotypical personality-type that historian Stanley M. Elkins had described nearly a decade earlier as Sambo. Elkins, in his controversial 1959 book *Slavery*, drew a dramatic parallel between the experiences of slaves on southern plantations and prisoners in Nazi concentration camps. He concluded that the personality patterns of both slaves and prisoners had been reshaped under the influence of powerful arbiters of life and death who functioned as "perverse father figures." Accepting Bruno Bettelheim's controversial interpretation of the behavior of concentration camp victims, Elkins portrayed the putative "dehumanization" of the Jewish prisoners as analogous to the putative "dehumanization" of the African American slaves. More concerned than any previous scholar with the slave personality-structure, he assumed that the "sanctions of the system were in themselves sufficient to produce a recognizable personality type"— the Sambo type. After a generation of slavery, he believed the conditioning process was simply a matter of raising children within the new framework of enforced infantilism. So horrendous were the psychological effects of slavery, according to Elkins, that slaves lost their sense of identity, became childlike, and adopted the values of their white masters. Slaves not only *played* Sambo, he concluded, they actually *became* Sambos. In time the *role* became the *self*.[48]

But it is not true that Styron's Nat Turner lives in Elkins's slave South. Styron borrows only Elkins's Sambo characterization, not his harsh portrayal of the slave plantations as "concentration camps." Styron places his Virginia slaves in a very different plantation setting, one more nearly drawn from the work of an earlier historian, Ulrich B. Phillips. Elkins had described slavery in the American South as "uniquely dehumanizing in its effects on the enslaved" and had asserted that "no other form of slavery so thoroughly deprived a slave of all the rights and responsibilities of humanity." In his introduction to the second edition of *Slavery*, Elkins's friend Nathan Glazer writes that American slavery was "the most awful the world has ever known." But Phillips's slave regime had been "a curious blend of force and concession, of arbitrary disposal by the master and self-direction by the slave, of tyranny and benevolence, of antipathy and affection." Phillips's slave regime had been "a school for civilizing savages," a beneficent institution for both master and slave. Phillips had set the classic pattern for the scholarly defense of slavery in an interpretation that dominated the subject until the 1950s. Styron, promiscuously mixing Phillips's stereotyped stage settings with Elkins's stock characters, depicts his Nat living in a far more complex and varied slave South than the one depicted by either Elkins or Phillips.[49]

The Ten had lumped Phillips with Elkins into what they term "the Elkins-Phillips-Styron dream," with little apparent understanding that Phillips's and Elkins's depictions of slavery are diametrically opposed to each other. To them Phillips was "the classic apologist for slavery," and Elkins was "the sophisticated modern apologist." Styron might claim to be "meditating on history," they wrote, "but we are not fooled. We know that he is really trying to escape history." To the Ten, Nat Turner's insurrection was the culmination of a long and continuing black drive for freedom, a tradition of both active and passive resistance to slavery. And so to them Styron's omission of that drive and that tradition amounted to a denial of the central theme of black history.[50]

Styron reacted to the charge that he ignored evidence of the historical Nat Turner's black wife with a forthright denial: "There is not a shred of contemporary evidence—not a hint, not a single statement either in the original 'Confessions' or in the few newspaper accounts—to show that Nat Turner had a wife." With characteristic verve, historian Eugene Genovese came to Styron's defense by attacking the Ten Black Writers. He noted that they had attached great importance to Nat Turner's references in Gray's "Confessions" to his parents and to his grandmother. "How incredible, then," he declared, "that he failed to mention his wife. Perhaps she existed, perhaps not; perhaps she had some importance in his life, perhaps not. We do not know." He said that "the slim thread of evidence—or gossip" for "Turner's alleged black wife" dated from a secondary account "written thirty years after his death." William Styron had therefore "not falsified history by ignoring her." Styron agreed: "Gene Genovese is absolutely right when he puts down this myth about Nat's wife— that's one of the most idiotic of the criticisms."[51]

The secondary source Genovese referred to was an 1861 essay in the *Atlantic Monthly* by Thomas Wentworth Higginson, a radical abolitionist from Massachusetts, who claimed to have obtained his information from "contemporary newspapers." According to Higginson, the historical Nat Turner had a wife Cherry Turner, a daughter, and one or two sons. All were sold off after the revolt. We know, Higginson said, "that Nat Turner's young wife was a slave; we know that she belonged to a different master from himself." And, Higginson said, there was "one thing more which we do know of this young woman: the Virginia newspapers state that she was tortured under the lash, after her husband's execution, to make her produce his papers." Styron, who had apparently not read Higginson, blamed the uproar on "a fanatic named Howard Myer," who had written a biography of Higginson. "Myer quotes Higginson as saying—this is in 1860—that Nat Turner had a wife. Total hearsay."[52]

Another secondary source that Styron was familiar with, however, was *The Southampton Slave Insurrection,* by William S. Drewry, who reported that "Nat's son, Redic, survived him." Despite its having been written by an "unreconstructed Virginian" nearly three-quarters of a century after the rebellion, Styron had explicitly considered *The Southampton Slave Insurrection* a "valuable" source of "considerable information and detail." Why he doubted Drewry in this instance but not others he did not attempt to explain.[53]

Genovese and Styron were mistaken that there was "not a shred of contemporary evidence" for the existence of Nat Turner's wife, nor was her existence merely a matter of "gossip" or "total hearsay." There was in fact a letter, apparently from Governor John Floyd, published in the Richmond *Whig,* September 17, 1831, stating that "I have in my possession some papers given up by his wife under the lash."[54]

On the question of Margaret Whitehead, Styron responded to his critics in *The Nation* that "Nat Turner *was* hung up on Margaret Whitehead, bashing her brains out because of the same hatred and love and despair that make Americans today as then all hopelessly hung up—black and white—one with the other, wedded inseparably by the error and madness of history." In an interview he declared that Nat Turner "desired her; he wanted her. She represented to him all sorts of unnameable things." He conceded that he could not prove it, but he insisted that the "psychological truth" of his portrayal "lies in the fact that one often wishes to destroy what one most earnestly desires." If Styron's Nat lusts after the flesh, he is hardly the only preacher to have done so, either in fiction or in fact.[55]

The Ten had been especially angered by Styron's calling up the stereotype of the black beast by emphasizing rape in the rebellion. Styron had portrayed the rebel Will as a madman. The Will of William Styron's *Confessions* is not the Will of Thomas Gray's *Confessions.* According to Gray, Nat testified that Will had insisted to him that he would obtain his liberty or "lose his life." He said "his life was worth no more than others, and his liberty as dear to him." "That was enough," Nat said to Gray, "to put him in full confidence."[56]

Certainly, as historian Winthrop Jordan notes, "if ever insurrectionary slaves in the United States had good opportunity for ravishing white women, it was during the Nat Turner rebellion in 1831." Yet no sexual incidents are mentioned in the record of the trial. In all the anguished outpouring of public horror called forth by the bloody rebellion, no newspaper at the time seems even to have hinted at rape or attempted rape on the part of the rebels. In the midst of all the shocked denunciations of the violence, a report in the Richmond *Constitutional Whig* went to the trouble of pointing out that "it is not believed that any outrages were offered to the females."[57]

Thirty years after the Southampton County rebellion, the erstwhile abolitionist Thomas Wentworth Higginson published a brief history of the insurrection in the *Atlantic Monthly*. He declared that during the rebellion one fear, though it must have racked "many a husband and father," had been groundless. He reminded his readers that the rebels "had been systematically brutalized from childhood; they had been allowed no legalized or permanent marriage; they had beheld around them an habitual licentiousness, such as can scarcely exist except in a Slave State; some of them had seen their wives and sisters habitually polluted by the husbands and the brothers of these fair white women." Yet, he wrote, he had searched "through the Virginia newspapers of that time in vain for one charge of an indecent outrage on a woman against these triumphant and terrible slaves." When white women were "absolutely in their power," these brutalized men did not seize the opportunity to retaliate in kind. They committed "no gratuitous outrage beyond the death-blow itself, no insult, no mutilation." Wherever they went they killed men, women, and children impartially, sparing "nothing that had a white skin." As Higginson put it, "Wherever they went, there went death, and that was all."[58]

Sixty-nine years after the Nat Turner revolt, William S. Drewry, a historian Styron would later describe as an "unreconstructed Virginian," discussed his own interviews with people who claimed to remember the days of terror. "Some say that victims were murdered and no further outrages committed," he wrote, "but this is in error." Shrouding his words in the polite euphemisms of the time, he declared that "women were insulted." He said he had been told that "Nat offered protection to one beautiful girl if she would consent to be his wife, but death was to this noble woman a blessing in comparison with such a prospect."[59]

The Ten had resented what they considered Styron's attempts to undercut Nat Turner's credentials as a heroic military commander. In Styron's *Confessions* Nat is made to say, "all strength had left me, my arms were like jelly"; and when he tries to kill he "missed by half a foot." According to Turner's own testimony to Gray, one of the rebels observed that the leader "must spill the first blood." Thus, "armed with a hatchet, and accompanied by Will, I entered my master's chamber." But, "it being dark, I could not give a death blow." Nat's hatchet glanced off Travis's head. "He sprang from the bed and called his wife," Nat told Gray; but "it was his last word," for "Will laid him dead, with a blow of his axe." At another house Nat chose a woman to be his victim. "I struck her several blows over the head, but not being able to kill her, as the sword was dull. Will turning around and discovering it, dispatched her also." Styron maintained that "it was quite clear to me that he was unable to kill. In his confession, he says more than once that the sword glanced off his head or that the sword was dull and he could not kill. Now this seems to me a patent evasion." As Genovese reads Turner's testimony, the rebel leader "hit a defenseless man on the head with a hatchet and could not kill him; he hit a woman on the head with a sword and could not kill her." According to the Ten, however, Nat failed to kill his master because it was dark and his hatchet glanced, and he failed to kill the woman because his sword was dull and light. Genovese notes wryly that "neither darkness nor inferior weapons kept his associates from doing better."[60]

The Ten had objected to Styron's portraying the caged Nat Turner as being rueful and penitent, contending that he went to his grave without remorse for what he had done. The Governor of Virginia had noted that all the insurrectionists "died bravely indicating no reluctance to lose their lives in such a cause." But Higginson, on whom the Ten had relied for other data, portrayed Nat after the murders in a manner remarkably similar to Styron's depiction:

> Now the blood was shed, the risk was incurred, his friends were killed or captured, and all for what? Lasting memories of terror, to be sure, for his oppressors; but, on the other hand, hopeless failure for the insurrection, and certain death for him. What a watch he must have kept that night! To that excited imagination, which had always seen spirits in the sky and blooddrops on the corn and hieroglyphic marks on the dry leaves, how full the lonely forest must have been of signs and solemn warnings! Alone with the fox's bark, the rabbit's rustle, and the screech-owl's scream, the self-appointed prophet brooded over his despair.

But according to Thomas Gray, who had asked Nat in prison, "Do you not find yourself mistaken now?" Nat had answered, "Was not Christ crucified?" Upon his arraignment, Nat refused to plead guilty, "saying to his counsel, that he did not feel so." Virginia authorities regarded the prisoner's appearance to be "not remarkable, his nose is

flat, his stature rather small, and hair very thin, without any peculiar-
ity of expression." Gray, on the other hand, said he looked upon Nat
Turner's "calm, deliberate composure, and my blood curdled in my
veins."[61]

The Ten did not find credible the last-minute confession of Styron's Nat that he would have spared at least one white person. According to them, the rebels had determined that "neither age nor sex
was to be spared," and they had not made any exceptions. But in fact,
as the governor of Virginia wrote to the governor of South Carolina,
Nat Turner did spare a family of poor whites: "They spared but one
family and that one was *so* wretched as to be in all respects upon a
par with them."[62]

The Ten did not write as temperate scholars seeking to set the
record straight with patient citations to verifiable evidence, but as
political activists, as clever polemicists who made their way through
Styron's novel with scathing distaste. Their discourse was marked by
an unnecessary tone of personal invective that embarrassed even
some of their allies. Their indictment of William Styron as a perpetra-
tor of fraud and deception was quite overt; they imputed to the author
not only a lack of historical or literary merit but also moral turpitude.
They professed to "catch him redhanded manipulating evidence," and
they accused him of deliberately deceiving the public about the true
nature of slavery in general and Nat Turner in particular. According
to the censorious Ten, Styron had created a character filled with his
own white neuroses and the degrading character traits of his own
white bigotry. According to them, his selection of "the types of psychological material which appear to emasculate and degrade Nat
Turner and his people" betrayed both "obvious" and "subtle" exhibi-
tions of white racist attitudes." According to them, Styron, as a white
Virginian raised in a racist society, "is not free from the impact of its
teachings." According to them, he "has not been able to transcend
his southern peckerwood background." In their opinion, Styron's *Confessions* was "a throwback to the racist writing of the 1930s and
1940s."[63]

According to Styron, Genovese's "counterattack" in the *New
York Review of Books* had "effectively demolished my critics." Not
only that, but he had done it "with such lofty outrage that the effect
was like that of a catharsis." Genovese, he believed, had "disposed of
the case once and for all." He had done no such thing. Despite the
strident, almost hysterical tone of their criticism, the Ten Black Writers had made a strong case against Styron's representation of Nat

Turner. Much of their indictment was on target in that Styron's book rested upon a weak historical foundation. Reading Styron's *Confessions*, one was uncomfortably aware of his having borrowed characters, events, and language from history without quite giving them vitality. Stripped of its layers of invented detail, much of the factual substance of Styron's *Confessions* stood rather painfully reduced.[64]

If Styron had failed at the challenge of creating a historically accurate Turner, what about the Ten Black Writers? Were they not also guilty of creating a Nat Turner for a specific audience? Were they not also guilty of projecting their own psychic needs upon their construction as surely as did William Styron? They had certainly corrected some of Styron's numerous errors of fact. And in cases in which Gray's *Confessions* lent itself to more than one interpretation, they certainly interpreted the evidence differently. But their version of history, like Styron's, was painfully ill-informed. They apparently entertained the delusion that historical research consisted of no more than reading *American Negro Slave Revolts,* Herbert Aptheker's 1937 master's thesis, ultimately published in 1966. In fact, their construction of Nat Turner did not even purport to rest upon historical sources so much as upon folkloric ones, upon an image they claimed to exist in "the living traditions of black America." This image is an invented tradition. It is certainly not supported by any evidence in the scores of collections or analyses of authentic field-recorded African-American oral tradition. Indeed, their construction of a powerful, commanding Nat Turner is far more nearly in the image of the Paul Bunyans and the frontier boasters of white folklore than in that of the great tricksters—Anansi, Buh Rabbit, and High John de Conquer—that have been so characteristic of African and African-American folklore. The tricksters, whether animal or human, overcome larger and more powerful critters not by using their physical force but by using their intellect.[65]

There is, to be sure, evidence about Nat Turner in both forms of the so-called slave narratives: the memoirs of escaped slaves and the interviews with ex-slaves conducted in the 1930s by the Federal Writers Project. But this evidence does not seem to have been used by either Styron or the Ten Black Writers, or indeed, by anyone else. It certainly does not provide much support for the constructions of either Styron or the Ten. In fact, if it could be verified, some of the evidence of the WPA interviews would seem to contradict both Styron and the Ten, and most other sources as well.

According to self-emancipated slave Henry Clay Bruce, the rebellion caused "no little sensation amongst the slaveholders." Allen Crawford, a former slave interviewed in 1937 in North Emporia, Virginia, described the rebellion vividly. "It started out on a Sunday night," he said. "Fust place he got to was his mistress' house. Said God 'dained him to start the fust war with forty men. When he got to his mistress' house he commence to grab him missus baby and he took hit up, slung hit back and fo'h three times. Said hit was so hard for him to kill dis baby 'cause hit had bin so playful setting on his knee and dat chile sho did love him. So third sling he went quick 'bout hit—killing baby at dis rap." The rebels then went to another house, according to Crawford, and "went through orchard, going to the house—met a school mistress—killed her."[66] Crawford's testimony—based on family memories of his Uncle Henry, who was hanged as one of the insurrectionists—differs from Gray's purported "Confessions of Nat Turner" and other sources that contend Nat Turner only killed Margaret Whitehead, a detail that plays a pivotal role in Styron's novel.

Another Virginia slave remembered well the fear of the white folks. According to Fannie Berry, "I can remember my mistress, Miss Sara Ann, coming to de window an' hollering, 'De niggers is arisin', De niggers is arisin', De niggers is killin' all de white folks—killin' all de babies in de cradle!'" Harriet Jacobs wrote in her memoirs, *Incidents in the Life of a Slave Girl*, that she thought it strange that the whites should be so frightened "when their slaves were so 'contented and happy'!"[67]

As news of Nat Turner's murderous foray spread, the slaveholders forbade their slaves to hold meetings among themselves. Charity Bowery, a former slave born in 1774 near Pembroke, North Carolina, recalled in an interview with abolitionist Lydia Maria Child published during the 1830s that "all the colored folks were afraid to pray in the time of old Prophet Nat. There was no law about it; but the whites reported it round among themselves that, if a note was heard, we should have some dreadful punishment; and after that, the low whites would fall upon any slaves they heard praying, or singing a hymn, and often killed them before their masters or mistresses could get to them." Nevertheless, as former slave James Lindsay Smith recalled, "notwithstanding our difficulties, we used to steal away to some of the quarters to have our meetings." Charity Bowery recalled a hymn from that period from the white hymnbooks:

A few more beatings of the wind and rain,
Ere the winter will be over—
Glory, Hallelujah!

Some friends has gone before me,—
I must try to go and meet them
Glory, Hallelujah!

A few more risings and settings of the sun,
Ere the winter will be over—
Glory, Hallelujah!

There's a better day a coming—
There's a better day a coming—
Glory, Hallelujah!

"They would't let us sing that," Bowery testified. "They would't let us sing that. They thought we was going to *rise*, because we sung 'better days are coming.'"[68]

The day following the insurrection, the Virginia militia was mustered to search the quarters of all slaves and free blacks. Harriet Jacobs said the militia planted false evidence to implicate some slaves in the rebellion. She claimed, "The searchers scattered powder and shot among their clothes, and then sent other parties to find them, and bring them forward as proof that they were plotting insurrection." Allen Crawford recalled that "Blues and Reds—name of soldiers— met at a place called Cross Keys, right down here at Newsome's Depot. Dat's whar they had log fires made and every one dat was Nat's man was taken bodily by two men who catch you and hold yer bare feet to dis blazing fire 'til you tole all you know'd 'bout dis killing." In the wake of the Turner insurrection, Henry Box Brown wrote in his memoirs, many slaves were "half-hung, as it was termed—that is, they were suspended from some tree with a rope about their necks, so adjusted as not quite to strangle them—and then they were pelted by men and boys with rotten eggs." The air was filled with shrieks and shouts. Harriet Jacobs said she "saw a mob dragging along a number of colored people, each white man, with his musket upraised, threatening instant death if they did not stop their shrieks." Jacobs could not contain her indignation. "What a spectacle was that for a civilized country!" she exclaimed. "A rabble, staggering under intoxication, assuming to be the administrators of justice!"[69]

According to Crawford, "Ole Nat was captured at Black Head Sign Post, near Cortland, Virginia—Indian town. He got away. So after a little Nat found dem on his trail so he went back near to the Travis place whar he fust started killing and he built a cave and made shoes in this cave. He came out night fur food dat slaves would give him from his own missus plantation." After about a month Nat Turner's hiding place was discovered, and he was taken into custody. Turner's captors, Crawford said, "brought him to Peter Edward's farm. 'Twas at this farm whar I was born. Grandma ran out and struck Nat in the mouth, knocking the blood out and asked him, 'Why did you take my son away?' In reply Nat said, 'Your son was as willing to go as I was.' It was my Uncle Henry dat they was talking about." Then, Crawford said, Virginia "passed a law to give the rest of the niggers a fair trial and Nat, my Uncle Henry, and others dat was caught was hanged."[70]

Charity Bowery recalled that "the brightest and best men were killed in Nat's time. Such ones are always suspected." After Nat Turner's revolt, slaveholders became much exercised over the question of what privileges—if any—they should grant to their slaves. Jamie Parker, a self-emancipated former slave, reported that the slaveholders finally decided that fewer privileges for slaves would afford "less cause for insurrections."[71]

Granting that Styron's Nat Turner is not the historical Nat Turner, and acknowledging that his exercise in blurring genres may have been misguided, even conceding that the author brought some of his troubles on himself by trying to wriggle out from under the "historical novel" label,[72] it would seem willful blindness not to reconsider the shallowness of evaluating a novel as though it were a historical monograph. With some misgivings about attempting literary pronouncements, one might at least say that the question of the book's ultimate standing is more likely to rest upon its literary qualities than upon its historical ones.

No one who has read Styron's earlier books will be surprised to find in *The Confessions of Nat Turner* persistent themes that have been at the center of his consciousness throughout his career. His novels are almost obsessively preoccupied with the polarities of power and submission, of authority and subservience, of being and nothingness; with conflicts between fundamentalism and skepticism; with the destruction of innocence by time and experience, with the loss of childhood's naive faith in an ordered and benevolent world; and, perhaps, above all, with the power of guilt and the possibility of redemption. His novels are all narrated in an almost biblical rhetoric of storytelling. His novels all reveal an intense and deeply religious sensibility. For Styron's protagonists to be saved, their existence demands justification by faith, whether faith in themselves or in something beyond self.[73]

Not only are Styron's persistent themes reiterated in his *Confessions*, but his Nat Turner is created in the image of the generic Styron hero-victim of the earlier novels, doomed to wrestle with the most profound existential questions. One can hardly miss the resemblance of Styron's Nat Turner to his Captain Mannix in *The Long March*, another awkward and unwilling rebel who defies the tyranny of another authoritarian institution, in his case the United States Marine Corps. "Even Mannix," Styron writes, "was aware that his gestures were not symbolic, but individual, therefore hopeless, maybe even absurd." One can hardly miss the resemblance of Styron's Nat Turner to his Cass Kinsolving in *Set This House on Fire*, who, like Nat, chooses being rather than nothingness. A would-be painter enslaved to alcoholism rather than to the Peculiar Institution, he is subjected to all sorts of public indignities by his boorish patron Mason Flagg in exchange for the liquor that helps him hang on. Feeling "sick as a dog inside my soul," but unable to figure out "where that sickness came from," he stumbles through a cycle of drunken depravity followed by spiritual retching in Styron's complex narrative of the terror of guilt and the horror of freedom. Ultimately, however, when Flagg rapes a young Italian girl, Cass kills him. "To choose between them," he says, "is simply to choose being, not for the sake of being, or even for the love of being, much less the desire to be forever—but in the hope of being what I could be for a time."[74]

In his first novel, *Lie Down in Darkness*, Styron evokes a world of complex, half-conscious feelings and perceptions of being and nonbeing. In a stunning Joycean interior monologue, his heroine-victim Peyton Loftis looks back over her life before she ends it. Locked in a stream of memories from which the sole escape is drowning in the airless void of time, she strips herself to what she calls "this lovely shell" of her naked body, and plunges out the window to her death on the street below. "Perhaps I shall rise at another time, though I lie down in darkness and have my light in ashes." Birds, symbolizing her sexual guilt and her yearning for freedom, haunt Peyton throughout the novel; and their wings rustle over her death.[75]

The predominant image of Peyton's last moments is drowning, but Styron also uses water as a symbol of rebirth. The strange epilogue of *Lie Down in Darkness* is dominated by the baptismal rites of Daddy Faith, an African American evangelist. Styron represents black Christians immersed and purified in the waters of life with a power and glory in dramatic contrast to the pity and terror of Peyton's plunge into death. Styron depicts the joy and faith of the black Christians (qualities conspicuously absent from the lives of his white characters) with great respect, even as he evokes the image of "a crazy colored preacher howling those tremendously moving verses from Isaiah 40."[76] It is an image, at least on the surface, not altogether unlike his "crazy colored preacher" revolutionary in *The Confessions of Nat Turner.*

The Ten Black Writers accused Styron of constructing a Nat Turner more autobiographical than historical, a Nat Turner representing his own character traits. According to them, the fictional Nat Turner embodied "a lot of Styron's own personality." According to them, "the voice in this confession is the voice of William Styron. The images are the images of William Styron. The confession is the confession of William Styron." They are not, of course, entirely mistaken. To some extent all fiction is autobiographical in that the created characters necessarily must come from the author's own experience and imagination. How could it be otherwise? The actions, attitudes, and emotions of any fictional character are first created within the consciousness of the writer. As Eudora Welty notes, "any writer is in part all of his characters. How otherwise would they be known to him, occur to him, become what they are?" Styron did not deny that he endowed his created Nat Turner with a personality very much like his own: "I wrote part of Nat as a projection of my own character, of course, like any creation of a writer, but he had to differ from the historical figure as we know him." The novel is written in what Styron calls "first person filtered through my own consciousness and my own thought processes. Actually, Nat is *me* in many of his responses to his life and environment."[77]

If Styron's Nat is autobiographical in his inward and most deeply felt responses, in his outward identity he is more nearly patterned after James Baldwin. Styron and Baldwin—the grandson of a slaveholder and the grandson of a slave—were close friends. From late fall of 1960 until early summer of 1961 Baldwin had lived in Styron's Connecticut studio. Although Baldwin's first novel, *Go Tell It on the Mountain,* was admired in literary circles, he was not yet a celebrity. A mutual friend had asked the Styrons to give Baldwin a place to stay, as he was having financial problems at the time. The "frightfully cold winter" of 1960 was "a good time for the Southern writer, who had never known a black man on intimate terms, and the Harlem-born writer, who had known few Southerners (black or white), to learn something, to learn something about each other." Baldwin inherited vivid images of slavery times passed down from his grandfather to his father. "Because he was wise," Styron wrote of his friend, "Jimmy understood the necessity of dealing with the preposterous paradoxes that had dwelled at the heart of the racial tragedy—the unrequited loves as well as the murderous furies." Styron, by his own testimony struggling to emancipate himself from "the prejudices and suspicions that a Southern upbringing engenders," considered himself "by far the greater beneficiary."[78]

Styron's Nat, at least in his outward experiences, would seem to be modeled as much on Baldwin's fictional heroes as on Baldwin himself. Baldwin represents rejection as the very essence of the black experience in America. But he approaches that essence by means of an extended metaphor of African Americans as the bastard children of American civilization. Johnny Grimes in Baldwin's *Go Tell It On the Mountain* is an archetypal image of the bastard black child. Rejected by whites for reasons he cannot understand, he is afflicted by an overwhelming sense of shame, the most destructive consequence of rejection. There must be something mysteriously wrong with him, Johnny reasons, to account for his rejection. Like Styron's Nat, Baldwin's Johnny undergoes an ecstatic and trance-like conversion experience. But not even African American religious ritual is free of the corrosive effects of racial rejection. As Baldwin notes, it is saturated in color symbolism. "Wash me, cried the slave to his Maker, and I shall be whiter, whiter than snow! For black is the color of evil; only the robes of the saved are white."[79]

Even the surreal spiritual visions of Styron's Nat have their counterparts in the religious fantasies of Baldwin's Johnny. As he lies before the altar in the depths of despair, Johnny's "ears were opened to this sound that came from the darkness. . . . It was a sound of rage and weeping . . . rage that had no language, weeping with no voice—which yet spoke now . . . of boundless melancholy, of the bitterest patience, and the longest night; of the deepest water, the strongest chains, the most cruel lash; of humility most wretched, the dungeon most absolute, of love's bed defiled, and birth dishonored, and most bloody, unspeakable, sudden death. Yes, the darkness hummed with murder. . . ?"[80] The victim of prolonged emotional rejection cannot escape its effects. The normal human personality will defend himself with hatred and dreams of vengeance. It may lose forever the capacity for love. Certainly Styron's Nat Turner would have had no difficulty understanding Baldwin's bitter and violent jazz drummer, Rufus Scott, the hero of book 1 of his *Another Country*, who sublimates his hatred by beating on the white skin of his drums.[81]

Styron may well have modeled Nat's relationship to an absent father on Baldwin's relationship to his own father and, perhaps even more, to his spiritual father, Richard Wright. According to Styron, "Jimmy once told me that he often thought the degradation of his grandfather's life was the animating force behind his father's apocalyptic, often incoherent rage." Baldwin's father, a Harlem preacher whom he described as "fanatical," left "a terrifying imprint on his son's life." He had died in 1943, and within a year Baldwin had met Wright for the first time. It is clear from his essays that the twenty-year-old Baldwin adopted the older man as a father figure. He also transferred his habit of defining himself in opposition to his father to the new relationship. Wright had elevated protest fiction to a new level, thus Baldwin would launch his own career with a rebellious essay called "Everybody's Protest Novel." Baldwin suppressed his own prophetic strain while Wright lived, but upon Wright's death in 1960, he could *become* his father. Baldwin soon ventured out on the lecture circuit, where "with his ferocious oratory," Styron notes, "he began to scare his predominantly well-to-do, well-meaning audiences out of their pants."[82]

Styron's Nat has other sources in African-American literary tradition. With no disposition to downplay significant differences between Richard Wright's Bigger Thomas and William Styron's Nat Turner, striking parallels are inescapable. Wright in *Native Son* creates in Bigger a protagonist who, like Nat, broods over the dissonance between subservience and freedom: "We black and they white. They got things and we ain't. They do things and we can't. It's just like living in jail. Half the time I feel like I'm on the outside of the world peeping in through a knot-hole in the fence." Like Nat, Bigger finds fulfillment in violently defying the legal and moral codes of the society that oppresses him. Like Nat, his victim is a kind-hearted young girl who is "friendly to Negroes." Wright represents Bigger's sickness as beyond the reach of mere kindness. His employers, the Daltons, are "good" people who hire him because they "want to give Negroes a chance." They are as innocent and as guilty as Styron's Samuel Turner. Styron's Nat and Wright's Bigger would seem to be violent twins, turning upon themselves in tautological fury, driven by what Baldwin called a "complementary faith among the damned," a faith that leads them at last to impel "into the arena of the actual those fantastic crimes of which they have been accused, achieving their vengeance and their own destruction through making the nightmare real."[83]

The most controversial component of Styron's *Confessions*, the component that infuriated his critics more than anything else, the component that called forth their most unmeasured epithets of contempt, was his representation of Nat's imagined sexual attraction to white women. "It was always a nameless white girl," he muses, "between whose legs I envisioned myself—a young girl with golden curls." He is particularly attracted to Margaret Whitehead, the only person he will actually kill personally. As Styron depicts it, Nat desires to fill his future victim with "warm milky spurts of desecration" or, in another instance, to repay the "pity" and "compassion" of a weak white woman with "outrageous spurts of defilement" and produce in her "the swift and violent immediacy of a pain of which I was complete overseer."[84]

If Nat's sexual attraction manifests white racist attitudes, however, what is one to make of Rufus Scott's love-hate desire for white women in Baldwin's *Another Country?* As he has sex with a white woman, Rufus fumes to himself that "nothing could have stopped him, not the white God himself nor a lynch mob arriving on wings. Under his breath he cursed the milk-white bitch and groaned and rode his weapon between her thighs." If Nat's sexual attraction manifests white racist attitudes, what is one to make of Bigger Thomas's rape and murder of Mary Dalton in Wright's *Native Son?* Even as he felt "a sense of physical elation" for this young woman who "did not hate him with the hate of other white people," even as he "watched her with a mingled feeling of helplessness, admiration, and hate," he thought to himself, "This little bitch!" He reflected that "she was white and he hated her." And after he had killed her, "he did not feel sorry for Mary; she was not real to him, not a human being." However unhistorical his construction of Nat Turner may have been, William Styron invested his protagonist with considerably more humanity and sensitivity than James Baldwin and Richard Wright bestowed upon Nat's counterparts. And if Nat's sexual attraction manifests white racist attitudes, what is one to make of the real life experiences of Eldridge Cleaver, for whom raping white women became a deliberate expression, both symptom and symbol of his dehumanization? "I became a rapist," he writes in *Soul on Ice*, published the year after Styron's *Confessions*. He raped, he said, "deliberately, willfully, methodically." He raped as a way of "getting revenge." He raped as "an insurrectionary act. It delighted me that I was defying and trampling upon the white man's law." [85]

Baldwin's Rufus Scott and Wright's Bigger Thomas are endowed with no such articulate self-understanding as Styron's Nat Turner. Wright stresses his protagonist's ignorance and his self-centered inability to perceive the humanity of whites: "To Bigger and his kind white people were not really people; they were a sort of gray natural force, like the stormy sky looming overhead." Killing Mary Dalton fills Bigger not with shame but with elation, with a sense of exhilaration, with a sense of purpose that transcends the meaninglessness of his former existence. "He had murdered and had created a new life for himself. It was something that was all his own. It was the first time in his life he had had anything that others could not take from him." [86]

A character in African-American fiction who *does* possess the kind of articulate self-understanding with which Styron endows his Nat Turner is the unnamed protagonist of Ralph Ellison's *Invisible Man*. But even he strikes out in a "frenzy" in response to an insult on a dark street, knocking his white tormenter to the ground. "In my outrage I got out my knife and prepared to slit his throat." Even Ellison's hero feels a generalized hatred of whites, believing in his soul that all black tragedies come from the same source. "You ache with the need to convince yourself that you do exist in the real world, that you're a part of all the sound and anguish, and you strike out with your fists, you curse and you swear to make them recognize you." [87] But Styron makes his Nat Turner a man capable of willed choice, and, therefore, he achieves a transcendence over the degradation of his enslavement. He shows that even in the worst circumstances a degraded state may be transcended. Does he really embody a stereotype more negative than the characters created by such African-American writers as Wright and Ellison?

However imperfectly Styron may have portrayed the Nat Turner revolt, few other American writers have made any effort to treat a slave insurrection at all. One who tried was Herman Melville. In some minor ways, Styron's novel echoes Melville's "Benito Cereno," the story of a shipboard slave rebellion, published in 1856. Like Melville, Styron is fascinated by the evil of slavery and what he sees as its inevitable connection with violence and corruption. But in Melville's slave rebellion there is still a memory of innocence. For Styron's Nat there is neither innocence nor redemption. From the corruptions of childhood, he acts out his damnation, moving hesitantly but relentlessly toward his revolutionary bloodbath. And Styron is different from Melville in another and more significant way. "Benito Cereno" is viewed entirely from a white perspective—that of the Yankee skipper Captain Amasa Delano. Styron at least tries to see Nat Turner's rebellion through Nat Turner's eyes. In the tragic encounter between sentimental and comic stereotypes, Melville seems as baffled by the behavior of his black rebels as is his protagonist. Delano is prepared to believe almost any evil of such a spiritually wasted European aristocrat as the slaveholder Benito Cereno. But the New Englander refuses to credit "the imputation of malign evil in man" to such simple and jolly primitives as he believes blacks to be. The fact that barbarous sadists lurk behind their masquerades makes the problem of slavery and slave revolts an exotic one for Melville, and makes "Benito Cereno" into a gothic horror tale.[88]

In the same year Harriet Beecher Stowe published her own fictional treatment of a slave revolt. *Dred* never had as much impact as her *Uncle Tom's Cabin*, with its melodramatic scenes of Eliza crossing the ice, the death of Little Eva, or Uncle Tom's brutal beating at the hands of Simon Legree. In *Dred* her rebellious slave protagonist is based in part on Nat Turner. But unlike Styron's Nat, Stowe's Dred is represented as a brutish madman, and his anticipated insurrection is prompted by a twisted perversion of biblical prophecy. Stowe is betrayed by her inability to construct believable black characters who are neither servile nor insane. She manipulates her plot so that Dred dies before receiving the heavenly sign that would precipitate the bloody insurrection. Thus, unlike Styron, she avoids having to consider either the deeper motivations or the deeper results of the revolution. And, unlike Styron, she opts for a sentimental ending in which her slaves and their white sympathizers go north to freedom.[89]

A more impressive novel about a slave conspiracy was Arna Bontemps's *Black Thunder*, published in 1936. Like Styron's Nat, Bontemps's protagonist is based on an actual historical figure, Gabriel Prosser, who led an abortive slave rebellion near Richmond in the summer of 1800, the year Nat Turner was born. In *Black Thunder* he constructed a narrative of men and women desperate enough to seek a revolution. "Anything that's equal to a gray squirrel," they believe, "want to be free. A wild bird what's in a cage will die anyhow, sooner or later," they conclude. "He'll pine hisself to death. He just as well break his neck trying to get out." Bontemps's Gabriel is "too old for joy, too young for despair." He is ready to write history with his life.

One may or may not lose one's life striking out for freedom; but since slavery is inevitably a living death, what have slaves to lose? Thus, like Nat Turner, Gabriel leads an uprising against the slaveholders. His insurrection, however, is sparked not by a longstanding hatred of enslavement carefully nurtured over the years (as in the case of Nat Turner), but by an immediate cause, by an unusually cruel punishment visited upon a mischievous slave. Also unlike Styron's Nat, Bontemps's Gabriel finds supporters not only within the slave community but also among free persons of color and even among some white sympathizers. And Gabriel's uprising comes much closer to success than did Nat Turner's. Only the intervention of a torrential rainstorm and a last-minute betrayal prevent the rebels from seizing Richmond. As in the case of Nat Turner, the rebellion is suppressed, the leaders are captured, and white Virginians visit blind and bloody retribution on the slaves. And the courageous but defeated hero Gabriel, like Nat Turner, pays for his love of freedom with his life. Unlike Styron's choice to write in the persona of Nat Turner, however, Bontemps chooses to tell Gabriel's story from a constantly shifting point of view, focusing in progressive chapters on the various participants, in the manner of John Dos Passos, forcing readers to collate the various perspectives themselves.[90]

William Styron might have spared himself considerable pain and humiliation had he fictionalized more rather than less. The inevitable accompaniment of Styron's choice was black fury. Without question the most offensive of Styron's faults to the Ten was his assuming the persona of Nat Turner, his writing about Nat Turner in the first person. From a literary standpoint no less than from an historical standpoint, Styron's choice was selfdefeating, fatally undermining the tragic potential of his novel.

It need not have been so. Styron has been (perhaps inevitably) compared to William Faulkner. But it was not one of Faulkner's books but Robert Penn Warren's *All the King's Men* that was the turning point in Styron's efforts to realize himself as a novelist: Styron had before him Warren, a distinguished example of how to avoid corrupting the construction of an historical figure with one's own personality. The book made an extraordinary, unforgettable impact on Styron when he first read it. "The book itself was a revelation and gave me a shock to brain and spine like a freshet of icy water," he wrote. "I had of course read many novels before, including many of the greatest, but this powerful and complex story embedded in prose of such fire and masterful imagery—this, I thought with growing wonder, this was what a novel was all about, this was *it*, the bright book of life, what writing was supposed to be." He completed the book, he said, "in a trance, knowing once and for all that I, too, however falteringly and incompletely, must try to work such magic."[91]

It is obvious that Warren's protagonist, Willie Stark, is modeled in some respects on the colorful Louisiana politician Huey Long. But as a novelist, Warren, while following the general outlines of Long's career, is free to create a Willie Stark who does not resemble Huey Long in every particular. Furthermore, in *All the King's Men* Warren assumes the persona not of Willie but of a failed history graduate student named Jack Burden. Some critics—noting that Warren never finished his Ph.D. either and that his first book was a pedestrian attempt at historical biography—find in Jack Burden more than a trace of Red Warren himself. In many of his vacillating responses to his life and his environment, Jack Burden is Robert Penn Warren. At least, so the argument goes. Whatever the source of Jack Burden's personality—and it should be remembered that Warren, after all, created the personalities of *all* his characters in the novel—the enhanced perspective of Burden's introspective consciousness strengthens rather than weakens *All the King's Men*.[92]

Not only did Styron have an obvious authorial model in Warren, he had an obvious candidate for the author's persona in the character of Thomas Gray, the lawyer to whom the historical Nat Turner dictated his jail cell "Confessions." Although he had once lived on an eight-hundred-acre estate worked by twenty-one slaves, young Thomas Gray by 1831 was disinherited and down to three hundred acres and one slave. He risked social ostracism to defend four of the insurrectionary slaves. Here was an inviting figure for Styron to endow with his own hesitations and vacillations, with his own ambivalence between an abstract commitment to justice and a very personal and concrete love for Virginia and its people. Here was an ambiguous but fascinating figure in whom to embody historical and literary anachronisms and contradictions.[93]

But ultimately neither historical nor literary considerations dictated Styron's choice to write of Nat Turner from within. One of the states of mind from which art may spring is an urgent sense of moral crisis. In "This Quiet Dust," an article he wrote for *Harper's* in 1965, two years before *The Confessions*, Styron reflected on what he thought and felt upon returning to the Virginia tidewater. The returning native saw much that he had missed before. "My boyhood experience," he wrote, "was the typically ambivalent one of most native Southerners, for whom the Negro is simultaneously taken for granted and as an object of unending concern." He had come to realize that "the Southern white's boast the he 'knows' the Negro" is not true. "An unremarked paradox of Southern life is that its racial animosity is really grounded not upon friction and propinquity but upon an almost complete lack of contact." But that lack of understanding would no longer suffice for a man of conscience in 1965. "To come to *know* the Negro," Styron concluded, "has become the moral imperative of every white Southerner." Thus his search for Nat Turner, his attempt "to re-create and bring alive that dim and prodigious black man," was his effort to respond to that moral imperative.[94]

How can the strange career of Nat Turner as man and as symbol be summarized? Styron's dilemma was the ambiguity of Nat Turner, and the dilemma is doubly ironic in Turner's appearing to be what he must but cannot become—a symbol rather than a human being. Styron's choice, to assume the persona of his protagonist, was a choice to treat his protagonist as a human being rather than as a symbol. If Styron's Nat is at times uncertain, he is hardly alone; many of the greatest leaders have hesitated. It is not difficult to think of either fictional or historical counterparts.

Much of the controversy over Styron's *Confessions* was characterized by rival sets of clichés. One set of them tiresomely reiterated Styron's failures of historical accuracy. The other tiresomely reiterated Styron's right as a novelist to make up his own characters and plots any way he wanted to. Each position was, in its own way, equally correct and equally irrelevant. Whatever the therapeutic value of such pronouncements, the issues were considerably more complex than either Styron, his attackers, or his defenders were willing to concede. Styron's imagination desired the novelist's freedom to create recalcitrant details rather than the historian's responsibility to uncover them. It is sometimes a source of great insight, sometimes of egregious error. Robert Penn Warren phrases it memorably, "the autonomy of the art is always subject to the recalcitrance of the materials," to which Ralph Ellison responds: "Yes. And I'm all for the autonomy of fiction; that's why I say that novelists should leave history alone." Efforts to recreate historical figures, Ellison says: "are *poison* to the novelist; he shouldn't bother them. Don't appropriate the names. Don't move into the historian's arena, because you can only be slaughtered there." Readers bring certain perspectives to their response to any book. Those informed by knowledge of the historical Nat Turner bring to Styron's *Confessions* a different cultural competence from those uninformed by any such knowledge, and thus a different reading position that allows them to activate the meaning of the book in ways beyond the reach of those whose cultural competence allows them to read the book only as fiction. As C. Vann Woodward noted in another connection, "Omniscience and mind reading are part of the novelist's license and are regularly used in writing of fictional characters without special cause for wonder." It is only "when the same license is used about real people, historical people we know a great deal about" that the "constant juxtaposition and confusion of the real and the imagined gives the historian chills and fever, whether or not he shares the entertainment enjoyed by the laity."[95]

Styron, like William Faulkner before him, endows his protagonist with contradictory characteristics. According to Ralph Ellison, Faulkner built upon "the Southern mentality" in which blacks were "dissociated" into "malignant" and "benign" stereotypes. Although Faulkner was "more willing perhaps than any other artist" to "seek out the human truth" hidden behind such stereotypes, his usual method was to create "characters embodying both." Similarly, Styron endows his protagonist with both benign and malignant characteristics, with elements from both prevailing stereotypes. But in some interesting ways his Nat Turner derives less from the stereotypes than from the wise old grandfather in Ellison's *The Invisible Man*, who counsels his grandson: "I want you to overcome 'em with yesses, undermine 'em with grins, agree 'em to death and destruction, let 'em swoller you till they vomit or bust wide open." Until the time is ripe, the very servility of Styron's Nat is the perfect pose for a revolutionary living with his head in the lion's mouth. As historian Willie Lee Rose attested, "at rock bottom" Styron's *Confessions* was "a sympathetic fictional exploration of the complex mind and heart of a revolutionary."[96]

Perhaps black intellectuals were justified in taking offense at Styron's choice as presumptive. It was not the task of white writers "to define Negro humanity," Ralph Ellison had observed earlier, "but to recognize the broader aspects of their own." Ellison's words were clear, and perhaps Styron should have heeded them. Granting the contributions of white historians to the field of black history, the Ten may still have had understandable cause for dissatisfaction. But surely the Ten's denunciation of what they called Styron's "unspeakable arrogance" for "daring to set down his own personal view of Nat's life" is an overreaction. Styron's "first mistake," the Ten declared, was "to attempt the novel." His "second mistake" was "to pretend to tell the story from the point of view of Turner." The second mistake, they said, "was a colossal error, one that required tremendous arrogance." But the fault of the author lay not in his arrogance. When his novel is viewed in the light of his persistent thematic concerns, Styron appears far less arrogant and far more admirable than when he was attempting ineptly to defend himself against unfair attacks. If he fails to create an historically accurate Turner, he constructs as a novelist a sympathetic revolutionary, a hero of "humanity and sensitivity" who balances a "resolve to liberate his people" with "doubt and foreboding about the means." Far from demeaning Nat Turner, by endowing his fictional creation with "a more impressive character," Eugene D. Genovese suggests, Styron "may well exaggerate Turner's virtues." Styron may be a faulty historian; but he is a novelist of high seriousness. And his willingness to take risks for moral purposes is worth any number of petty perfectionists.[97]

For Styron his choice to try to create Nat Turner from what he called "a sense of withinness," from an "intensely 'inner' vantage point," his choice to try to see slavery through the eyes of Nat Turner in order to assume the "moral imperative" of every white Southerner to make good his claim to "understand the Negro"—was absolutely central. Conceding that he might very well have been trying to redress an imbalance in his own life, it is important to remember that in his first novel, *Lie Down in Darkness,* he represented a woman's depression partly through her own consciousness, and in his 1979 novel, *Sophie's Choice,* he represented the Holocaust partly through the consciousness of a Polish Catholic. Styron's struggle to achieve racial understanding was more characteristic and more admirable, and his measure of success was more precarious than has been generally recognized. In *Confessions* Styron's choice was an act of willed empathy not only with Nat Turner but also with such writers as Ralph Ellison and Richard Wright, who had regarded African-American history as existing not in a vacuum but within the overall pattern of American history. Styron himself had indicated of Nat Turner, "The natural working out of his life was symbolic—a metaphor for most of Negro life, I guess." But Wright had gone further. "The history of the Negro in America is the history of America written in vivid and bloody terms," he had insisted. "The Negro is *America's* metaphor."[98]

Toni Morrison in her *Playing in the Dark* stresses the importance of efforts to look into "the mind, imagination, and behavior of the slaves." But the "sense of how Negroes live and how they have so long endured," according to James Baldwin, has long been "hidden" from white Americans. The barriers to achieving that sense are formidable, Baldwin wrote in 1951, declaring that for white writers to comprehend the qualities of black life, white psychology "must undergo a metamorphosis so profound as to be literally unthinkable." At about the same time William Faulkner expressed a strikingly similar reservation: "It is easy enough," he wrote, "to say glibly, 'If I were a Negro, I would do this or that.' But a white man can only imagine himself for the moment a Negro; he cannot be that man of another race and griefs and problems." If, in *The Confessions of Nat Turner*, Styron was unable to "be that man of another race," if he fell short of achieving that "sense of how Negroes live and how they have so long endured," it was not enough merely to deplore his difficulties. That he made the effort, and that he made it in his characteristically ambitious fashion, was a deeply moral and deeply heroic choice. If, in *The Confessions of Nat Turner*, Styron fails in painful ways, who can be grateful that white writers—nor do black writers turn their talents to white subjects—make no further effort at fictional realization of African-American life? Have we not rung down a curtain of literary segregation more absolute than any political one?[99]

Sitting chained in his cell, Styron's Nat Turner ponders all he has done, all he has felt and suffered before his life is taken from him on the gallows, as Peyton Loftis in his *Lie Down in Darkness* ponders her life before taking it herself by plunging out the window to the street below. They speak to the deepest perceptions of the human condition, to a vision of tragic ambiguities and ironic necessities, to ecstatic moments of *being*, all the while surrounded by the terror of the timeless void. To have understood Nat Turner's tragedy in somewhat the same terms that Richard Wright, Ralph Ellison, and James Baldwin have understood the African-American experience is a considerable achievement. Despite Styron's difficulties, *The Confessions of Nat Turner* is a contribution of lasting literary value.[100]

"Ultimately," historian Joel Williamson has shown, "there is no race problem in the South, or in America, that we, both black and white, do not make in our minds."[101] Thus, whatever his novel's historical and literary shortcomings, William Styron may have achieved a usable historical image of Nat Turner after all, an image not of the powerful and peerless leader but of the potential for hate— and the potential for love—in everyone. Perhaps, as Edward Gibbon understated of another convulsion, "this awful revolution may be usefully applied to the instruction of the present age." And perhaps—in some strange, undefinable way, some way unfathomable by any ideology presently known, but in some way simply bestowed by the compassion of art—Nat Turner's symbolic ashes may yet give forth light.

Notes

Introduction

1. I should note, as an exception, that Susan Eacker's essay was first a paper written for a graduate seminar of mine at Miami University, but I played no role in her finding a place among the Webb lectures.

2. "The Center Does Not Hold" and "There Was No King in Israel," the penultimate and final chapters of Peter Novick, *That Noble Dream: The "Objectivity Question" and the American Historical Profession* (Cambridge: Cambridge University Press, 1988), 522–629.

3. Jean-Paul Sartre, *Words*, trans. Irene Clephane (London: Hamish Hamilton, 1964), 125. Cf. Peter Burke, ed., *A New Kind of History: From the Writings of Lucien Febvre* (London: Routledge and Kegan Paul, 1973).

4. Jefferson Humphries, ed., *Southern Literature and Literary Theory* (Athens: University of Georgia Press, 1990).

5. I draw here on Nicholas Phillipson, *Hume* (London: Weidenfeld and Nicolson, 1989), 44–46; the original texts are David Hume, *A Treatise of Human Nature*, ed. Ernest C. Mossner (1739–40: Harmondsworth: Penguin, 1969), 233–34, 257, 300, 316.

What's So Funny?

1. Augustus Baldwin Longstreet, "The Horse-swap," in *Georgia Scenes: Characters, Incidents, etc. in the First Half-Century of the*

Republic, by a Native Georgian (1835; New York: Harper and Brothers, 1840), 23, 24, 32, 33.

2. Joseph G. Baldwin, "An Equitable Set-Off," in *The Flush Times of Alabama and Mississippi: A Series of Sketches*, with an introduction and notes by James H. Justus (1853; Baton Rouge: Louisiana State University Press, 1987), 273, 74, 75.

3. Mark Twain, *Roughing It* (1872; New York: Penguin, 1981), 197–99, 202.

4. There is a great deal of literature on the market revolution. For a controversial single-volume survey, see Charles Sellers, *The Market Revolution: Jacksonian America, 1815–1846* (New York: Oxford University Press, 1991). A very different interpretation, but one that covers the same process of economic development and its effects on American society and culture, may be found in Robert H. Wiebe, *The Opening of American Society: From the Adoption of the Constitution to the Eve of Disunion* (New York: Alfred A. Knopf, 1984). For an interesting study of the relationship between a developing economy and reading, see Ronald J. Zboray, *A Fictive People: Antebellum Economic Development and the American Reading Public* (New York: Oxford University Press, 1993).

5. Alan Gribben, "Mark Twain Reads Longstreet's *Georgia Scenes*," in *Gyascutus: Studies in Antebellum Southern Humorous and Sporting Writing*, ed. James L. W. West (Atlantic Highlands, N.J.: Humanities Press, 1978), 103–111. Kenneth S. Lynn, *Mark Twain and Southwestern Humor* (Boston: Little, Brown, 1959), 167. The popular Crockett Almanacs published several variations of the horse-swap tale. See for example "Buying a Horse" (1839), reprinted in Michael A. Lofaro, ed. *The Tall Tales of Davy Crockett: The Second Nashville Series of Crockett Almanacs, 1839–1841* (Knoxville: University of Tennessee Press, 1987), 19.

6. Michael T. Gilmore, *American Romanticism and the Marketplace* (Chicago: University of Chicago Press, 1985).

7. For example, William Gilmore Simms, *Richard Hurdis: Or, The Avenger of Blood* (1838), in later editions entitled *Richard Hurdis: A Tale of Alabama*.

8. Johanna Nicol Shields, "A Sadder Simon Suggs: Freedom and Slavery in the Humor of Johnson Hooper," *Journal of Southern History* 56 (Nov., 1990): 641–64.

9. T. W. Lane, "The Thimble Game," in *Polly Peablossom's Wedding: and Other Tales*, ed. T. A. Burke (Philadelphia: T. B. Peterson and Brothers, 1851), 36. Johnson Jones Hooper, *Adventures of*

Captain Simon Suggs, with a foreword by Clyde N. Wilson (1845; Nashville: J. S. Sanders and Co., 1993), 118. George Washington Harris, *Sut Lovingood: Yarns Spun by a Nat'ral Born Durn'd Fool* (New York: Dick and Fitzgerald, 1867), 30. "Mike Hooter's Fight with a 'Bar'" by H. [William C. Hall, 1849] in *Humor of the Old Deep South*, ed. Arthur Palmer Hudson (Port Washington, N.Y.: Macmillan, 1936, 1970), 115. On the Mike Hooter stories, see John Q. Anderson, "Mike Hooter—The Making of a Myth," in *The Frontier Humorists: Critical Views*, ed. M. Thomas Inge (Hamden, Conn.: Anchor Books, 1975), 197–207.

10. Joan Jensen, *Loosening the Bonds: Mid-Atlantic Farm Women, 1750–1850* (New Haven: Yale University Press, 1986). Jeanne Boydston, *Home and Work: Housework, Wages, and the Ideology of Labor in the Early Republic* (New York: Oxford University Press, 1990). Christopher Morris, *Becoming Southern: The Evolution of a Way of Life, Vicksburg and Warren County, Mississippi 1770–1860* (New York: Oxford University Press, 1995).

11. Longstreet, "The 'Charming Creature' as a Wife," in *Georgia Scenes*, 108–46. Longstreet in general portrays women as silly, childish, meddlesome, and superficial. He generally disparages marriage. In "The Dance" he describes what he believes is an exceptional woman, who "possessed a lovely disposition, which even marriage could not spoil" (p. 19). On the place of women in these stories, see William E. Lenz, "The Function of Women in Old Southwestern Humor: Rereading Porter's *Big Bear* and *Quarter Race* Collections," *Mississippi Quarterly* 46 (Fall, 1993), 589–600. On consumerism and peddlers, see Fred Mitchell Jones, *Middlemen in the Domestic Trade in the United States, 1800–1860* (Urbana: University of Illinois Press, 1937); Lewis Atherton, "Itinerant Merchandizing in the Antebellum South," *Bulletin of the Business Historical Society* 19 (1945): 35–59; Elizabeth A. Perkins, "The Consumer Frontier: Household Consumption in Early Kentucky," *Journal of American History* 78 (Sept., 1991): 486–510; David Jaffee, "Peddlers of Progress and the Transformation of the Rural North, 1760–1860," *Journal of American History* 78 (Sept., 1991): 511–35.

12. Lane, "Thimble Game," 29, 36. In this story a man goes to town to sell cotton because his wife desires a number of manufactured items, yet, Lane tells us, men once pushed to market by their wives immediately "lay aside their 'copperas-coloureds,' fabrics of the wife's or daughter's loom, and purchase a new suit of '*store-clothes.*'" See also Harris, "Sut's New Fangled Shirt," in *Sut Lov-*

ingood, 30; "Jones' Fight: A Story of Kentucky," by A North Alabamian [Thomas Kirkman?] and "Billy Warrick's Courtship and Wedding: A Story of 'The Old North State'," by A Country Lawyer, both in *The Big Bear of Arkansas*, ed. William T. Porter (1845), 32–41, 90–105.

13. Lane, "Thimble Game," 30, 40. Harris, "Blown Up with Soda," and "Rare Ripe Garden-Seed," in *Sut Lovingood*, quote from p. 79. See also "Rare Economy," (1841) in *Tall Tales*, 4–6.

14. Hall, "Mike Hooter's Bar Story," by H. [William C. Hall, 1850] in *Humor*, 118. Lane, "Thimble Game," 28–29. Longstreet, *Georgia Scenes*, especially "The Ball," pp. 160–74.

15. Hooper, *Simon Suggs*, 14, 69, 70, 74. On Mark Twain's representation of slaves as naïve victims, see, for example, *Adventures of Huckleberry Finn*, chapter 8, in which Jim explains to Huck how he was once rich but lost his fourteen-dollar fortune speculating in bad stocks and banks. Slaves very rarely appear in the forefront of stories by antebellum Southern writers, yet readers are generally made aware of their presence. Louis Rubin explained the reticence of Southern writers to discuss slavery, or generally to probe their society in much depth, as a product of a social context "all too flawed in its design and grounded upon an attitude toward a certain segment of the population that involved grave injustice and inhumanity." Thus, Rubin concluded, Southern literature from the slavery period was superficial. Closer readings reveal otherwise. On the barely visible, yet very significant, presence of slavery within, or perhaps beneath, the world of Simon Suggs, for example, see Shields, "Simon Suggs."

16. Peter Temin, *The Jacksonian Economy* (New York: W. W. Norton, 1969), 29–44.

17. Hall, "Mike Hooter's Fight," 116. "Scenes on Deer Creek and the Sunflower," by The Turkey Runner [Alexander G. McNutt] *The Spirit of the Times* (Apr. 20, 1844), 91. Hooper, *Simon Suggs*, 141–48. On McNutt see Elmo Howell, "Governor Alexander G. McNutt of Mississippi: Humorist of the Old Southwest," *Journal of Mississippi History* 35 (May, 1973): 153–65.

18. Hooper, *Simon Suggs*, 42–68, 118–33.

19. "A Quarter Race," by Mr. Snooks [Thomas Kirkman], *New York Spirit of the Times* 6 (July 9, 1836), 162. Republished in William T. Porter, ed. *A Quarter-Race in Kentucky and Other Sketches* (1846), and again in T. B. Thorpe, ed. *Major Thorpe's Scenes in Arkansas: Containing the Whole of the Quarter Race in Kentucky; and Bob Herring, the Arkansas Bear Hunter, As Well As Cupping the Sternum, Playing Poker in Arkansas, and Other Sketches Illustrative*

of Scenes, Incidents, and Characters, throughout "The Universal Yankee Nation" (1858). Lynn, *Mark Twain*, 76.

20. Lynn, *Mark Twain*, 61–76.

21. Longstreet, *Georgia Scenes*, 6–21.

22. Longstreet, *Georgia Scenes*, 160–74. In a humorous sketch about a poor North Carolina farmer's discovery of the social value of money, the lesson William Gilmore Simms has his hero learn is, of course, ironic: "Then I considered all about 'capital'; and it growed on me, ontil I begin to see that a man might hev good legs and arms and thighs, and a good face of his own, and yit not be a parfect and proper man a'ter all!" Simms's irony would not have been lost on Augustus Baldwin Longstreet. William Gilmore Simms, "How Sharp Snaffles Got His Capital and Wife," *Harper's New Monthly Magazine* (Oct., 1870), reprinted in *Stories of the Old South: Southern Fiction from Some of Our Greatest Storytellers*, eds. Ben Forkner and Patrick Samway (New York: Penguin, 1989), 388–428, quote from p. 402.

23. Kenneth Lynn first characterized antebellum Southern humorists as supporters of the Whig Party and its political philosophy. Though his characterization does not apply to all such writers, it certainly describes Kirkman accurately. Lynn, *Mark Twain*, pp. 55–72, 76.

24. Shields, "Simon Suggs," discusses how the lack of social and moral structures in *Simon Suggs* served to reinforce the commitment of individual readers to moral standards of conduct.

25. Literary critic David S. Reynolds has called Hooper, Baldwin, and Harris "subversive humorists," because they challenged traditional social values. That American readers were ready to be challenged is suggested by sales figures. In 1844, its first year in print, *Simon Suggs* sold ten thousand copies, and went through eleven editions over the next decade. David S. Reynolds, *Beneath the American Renaissance: The Subversive Imagination in the Age of Emerson and Melville* (New York: Alfred A. Knopf, 1988), 453–55.

26. Harris, "Sut Lovingood's Daddy, Acting Horse," in *Sut Lovingood*. Though born in 1814, a year before Hooper, Harris published his first Sut Lovingood story in 1854, more than a decade after the appearance of Hooper's first tale of Simon Suggs. Not until 1867 did the first collection of Sut Lovingood yarns appear. Not surprisingly, Harris's stories seem more distant from the modernizing world in which he wrote than do the stories published earlier by Hooper.

27. Lynn, *Mark Twain*, 174–79.

28. Authors such as Thomas Bangs Thorpe, born in the North

where market development was more advanced, also wrote nostalgically about a pristine, premarket old Southwest of giant bears and larger-than-life, though quaint, hunters and boatmen, who lived by simple, natural laws. Thorpe began what has become known as "The Big Bear" school of literature, which, like the Davy Crockett Almanacs of the same period, captured the imagination of eastern readers thoroughly ensconced in a modernizing society. He said very little about economy, never confused, as did Hooper and Baldwin, the values of the backwoods with those of an urbanizing and industrializing society, and so, like Twain, never challenged either within their historical context. Indeed, Thorpe was representative of eastern writers who, as historian Michael Fellman has argued, delegitimized the West to prepare it for its conquest by an expanding American, especially Northern, capitalist economy and society. Michael Fellman, "Alligator Men and Cardsharpers: Deadly Southwestern Humor," *Huntington Library Quarterly* 49 (1986): 307–23.

29. William Faulkner, "Spotted Horses," in *Three Famous Novels* (New York: Vintage, 1961), quotes from pp. 4, 22, 28, 48–49.

30. Faulkner, "Spotted Horses," 12, 14. In *The Sound and the Fury* Faulkner also wraps the tragic story of Jason in the humor of Jason's deeply bitter sarcasm. Jason, though confident he is the only member of the Compson family who maintains control over his life, is utterly at the mercy of the cotton exchange that is slowly destroying him.

A "Dangerous Inmate" of the South

An earlier version of this manuscript was presented to the Society for Historians of the Early American Republic during their annual meeting at the University of North Carolina, Chapel Hill, on July 24, 1993. I am indebted to Michael O'Brien, who gave freely of his time and talents as a fine editor during several drafts of this earlier paper. I also appreciate the formal comments on this work made by Nancy Hewitt at the Chapel Hill conference. In addition, I have many Marys to thank for their encouragement and assistance: Mary Cayton, Mary Frederickson, and Mary Kelley.

1. Actually, as Nancy Hewitt reminded me, although the Grimké sisters may have been cast by historians as the first women to publicly condemn slavery, both Maria Stewart and Francis Wright had taken up the cause of women and of the slave before the Grimkés. Still, as Hewitt stated in her written comments on this essay, "Stewart was an unschooled African American [and] Fanny Wright was a

foreigner and a fanatic. Both were too easily dismissed, by their contemporaries and ours."

2. This is not to say that historians have not dealt with the experiences of Southern women, black and white, under the plantation system. Among the wide number of works on that topic, see especially, Catherine Clinton, *The Plantation Mistress: Women's World in the Old South* (New York: Pantheon, 1982); Elizabeth Fox-Genovese, *Within the Plantation Household: Black and White Women of the Old South* (Chapel Hill: University of North Carolina Press, 1988), esp. 37–99; Eugene Genovese, "Our Family, White and Black: Family and Household in the Southern Slaveholder's World View," in *In Joy and Sorrow: Women, Family and Marriage in the Victorian South, 1830–1900,* ed. Carol Bleser (New York: Oxford University Press, 1991); Suzanne Lebsock, *The Free Women of Petersburg: Status and Culture in a Southern Town, 1784–1860* (New York: W. W. Norton and Co., 1984). While all of these authors discuss the relative positions of white women vis-à-vis their African-American contemporaries, none, save Clinton, takes the position that on the grounds of ideology, if not the actual terrain of the plantation, there was a common thread of patriarchal oppression linking women of both races. Both Fox-Genovese and Genovese, for example, favor a class-based analysis of plantation relations, thus downplaying the force of the white women/slave analog. Eugene Genovese articulates his position most forcefully in *The World the Slaveholders Made,* where he "affirms the priority of a class interpretation" of slavery against either a racial or sexual one. See Eugene Genovese, *The World the Slaveholders Made* (New York: Pantheon Books, 1969), 103.

3. Stephanie McCurry, "The Two Faces of Republicanism: Gender and Proslavery Politics in Antebellum South Carolina," *Journal of American History* 78 (Mar., 1992): 1251–52.

4. Joan W. Scott, "Rewriting History," in *Behind the Lines: Gender and the Two World Wars,* ed. Margaret Higonnet (New Haven: Yale University Press, 1987), 28–29. Although Scott is concerned principally with a linguistic analysis of official policy pronouncements on war, the striking similarities between gender and the discourse on war in her work and that of slavery in the present essay should become apparent.

5. Sarah M. Grimké, "Letters on the Equality of the Sexes and the Condition of Woman," [1837], reprinted in *The Public Years of Sarah and Angelina Grimké: Selected Writings, 1835–1839,* ed. Larry Ceplair (New York: Columbia University Press, 1989), 212.

6. Louisa M. McCord, "Enfranchisement of Woman," [1852], reprinted in *All Clever Men Who Make Their Way: Critical Discourse in the Old South*, ed. Michael O'Brien (Fayetteville: University of Arkansas Press, 1982), 344.

7. Elizabeth Fox-Genovese, *Within the Plantation Household: Black and White Women of the Old South* (Chapel Hill: University of North Carolina Press, 1988), 144, 288. Fox-Genovese claims that Southern women writers, unlike Northern female writers of the sentimental novel, "displayed their class loyalties by never consciously developing a distinct female genre." If this were so (and recent scholarship on women writers of the Old South suggests otherwise), then the reason may have more to do with their sex than their class, since women writers, unlike their male counterparts, could not afford to draw attention to their gender "infirmity." As Fox-Genovese herself points out, "publication could not be separated from unladylike self-display." See *Within the Plantation Household*, 246.

8. Fox-Genovese admits to this prior self-restraint by female authors in her discussion of Harriet Jacobs, author of *Incidents in the Life of a Slave Girl*, when she claims that Jacobs, "like slaveholding women who kept diaries or journals, shaped her presentation of herself to conform, at least in part, to the expectations of her intended readers." See Fox-Genovese, *Within the Plantation Household*, 376.

9. See Mary Kelley's "literary domestics," for example, who "believed in the dictum that woman's place was in the home as wife and mother, [but] nevertheless had stepped into a public arena traditionally ruled by men and had achieved a distinctive measure of success there." See Mary Kelley, *Private Woman, Public Stage: Literary Domesticity in Nineteenth-Century America* (New York: Oxford University Press, 1984), 7. Like her Northern sisters, Anne Goodwyn Jones claims that the woman writer of the South also experienced an "anxiety of authorship," which was played out in their novels as a "split between two sets of values, corresponding to the private and public selves of their southern women authors." Anne Goodwyn Jones, *Tomorrow is Another Day: The Woman Writer in the South, 1859–1936* (Baton Rouge: Louisiana State University Press, 1981), 39–40.

10. The choice of fiction itself, as Anne Goodwyn Jones has noted, was one of the "masks" of the nineteenth-century woman novelist. The genre allowed the female novelist to speak through the mask of many characters, making it difficult to discern the true authorial voice. Another subterfuge of fiction, as Steven Stowe has

pointed out, is that "novel writing had no means of permitting a woman to make a plain judgment or a sustained self-scrutiny—two risky, strong-minded activities." Therefore, McCord's choice of non-fiction as her hallmark was, in this sense, a bit more risky. It is also another similarity she shared with the Grimkés. See Steven M. Stowe, "City, Country, and the Feminine Voice," in *Intellectual Life in Antebellum Charleston,* eds. Michael O'Brien and David Moltke-Hansen (Knoxville: University of Tennessee Press, 1986), 315. Typically, the mimetic formula of the domestic or sentimental novel went like this: female nonconformity equals tragedy as lesson equals female conformity. As we shall see, McCord had already disabused herself of the temptation of testing the waters of female unconventionality, convinced as she was of the storm surge of male power that would leave the more naive female nonconformist struggling back to the safety of shore.

11. Jones, *Tomorrow is Another Day,* 25.

12. Historians have cited a variety of factors in helping to spawn this proslavery offensive, which began in earnest in the 1830s. They include South Carolina's nullification crisis, the proliferation in the South of abolitionist literature from the North, and the growing Southern fear of slave insurrection. For further elaboration see McCurry, "The Two Faces of Republicanism," in *The Ideology of Slavery: Proslavery Thought in the Antebellum South, 1830–1860,* ed. Drew Gilpin Faust (Baton Rouge: Louisiana State University Press, 1981), esp. 9–10; James Oscar Farmer, *The Metaphysical Confederacy: James Henry Thornwell and the Synthesis of Southern Values* (Macon, Ga.: Mercer University Press, 1986), esp. 24–25.

13. George Fitzhugh, "Southern Thought," in *The Ideology of Slavery,* 293.

14. For a discussion of the syncretism of secular and sacred defenses of slavery see Faust, ed., *The Ideology of Slavery* (esp., her introduction), and Farmer, *The Metaphysical Confederacy.*

15. Aristotle quoted in Rosemary Agonito, *History of Ideas on Women: A Sourcebook* (New York: Perigee Books, 1977), 52.

16. George Fitzhugh to George Frederick Holmes, Apr. 11, 1855, in Farmer, *The Metaphysical Confederacy,* 112–13; George Fitzhugh, *Sociology for the South,* quoted in Eugene Genovese, *The World the Slaveholders Made: Two Essays in Interpretation* (New York: Pantheon Books, 1969), 195.

17. William Harper, "Memoir on Slavery," *Southern Literary Journal* 3 (Jan., 1838): 161–74 (quotation on p. 72).

18. Harper, "Memoir on Slavery," 68.

19. Lacy Ford, Jr., for example, traces the yeoman's willingness to cohere around slavery to threats articulated by men such as William Trescot that "where there are no black slaves, there must be white ones." Thus slavery found favor with the South's nonelites "not [in] the planter ideal or the slaveholding ideal but the old country republican ideal of personal independence, given peculiar fortification by the use of black slaves." See Lacy K. Ford, Jr., *Origins of Southern Radicalism: The South Carolina Upcountry, 1800–1860* (New York: Oxford University Press, 1988), 361. Other historians such as Michael Wayne question whether slavery did "in fact secure liberty and advance equality among those who were free" and find in the historical record that many nonslaveholders, in fact, struggled against the hegemony of the ruling planter elite. Michael Wayne, "Social Underpinnings of Proslavery Ideology," *Journal of American History* 3 (Dec., 1990): 840.

20. Thomas Dew, *Review of the Debate in the Virginia Legislature of 1831 and 1832* (1832; reprint, Westport, Conn.: Negro Universities Press, 1920), 36.

21. Gerda Lerner, "Reconceptualizing Difference Among Women," *Journal of Women's History* 1 (Winter, 1990): 110. Extending her analysis to antebellum America, Lerner finds a comparable situation between white and black women of all classes, at least when it comes to political, legal, and educational rights. Adopting tenets of English common law, for example, legal strictures in the South (as well as the North) prevented both slaves and white married women from acquiring property or from making economic claims on their own labor, restrictions not placed on free blacks or single or widowed white women.

22. Clinton, *The Plantation Mistress*, 35.

23. Angelina E. Grimké, "An Appeal to the Women of the Nominally Free States," [1837], reprinted in ed. Ceplair, *The Public Years*, 132. Bruce Collins, for example, argues, that "the language of complaint in which women compared their lot to the slave ... merely reflected common usage [since] slavery served as a metaphor for degradation and defeat in a variety of complaints." This may be so, but it does not alter the fact that women must have felt "degradation and defeat" in order to express such sentiments. See Bruce Collins, *White Society in the Antebellum South* (London: Longman, 1985), 132–33.

24. For early biographies of Louisa McCord, see Jessie Melville Fraser, "Louisa C[heves]. McCord" (master's thesis, University of

South Carolina, 1919); and Margaret Farrand Thorp, *Female Persuasion: Six Strong-Minded Women* (New Haven: Yale University Press, 1949). As Susan Harris has written, "the desire for an education is one of the most common themes evinced in nineteenth-century women's literature; throughout, moreover, there is a sense that knowledge is power, definition; a chance to BE SOMEBODY." Susan K. Harris, *Nineteenth-Century American Women's Novels: Interpretative Strategies* (Cambridge: Cambridge University Press, 1990), 27. Women's expression for a well-rounded education was not just a theme in literature, but a real-life longing as well. Like McCord, Sarah Grimké would also feel that she had been short shrifted academically by not receiving the same education as her male siblings. In her later years, for example, the elder Grimké sister would write: "In vain I entreated permission to go hand and hand with my brothers through their studies. The only answer to my earnest pleadings was 'You are a girl—what do you want with Latin and Greek, etc.? You can never use them,' accompanied sometimes with a smile, sometimes with a sneer." Elizabeth Ann Bartlett, ed. *Sarah Grimké: Letters on the Equality of the Sexes and Other Essays* (New Haven: Yale University Press, 1988), 114.

25. Louisa Cheves [McCord] to Langdon Cheves, Jr., Oct. 7, 1839, Cheves Family Papers, South Caroliniana Library, Columbia, S. C. (hereinafter SCL). Again, the analogous early experiences of McCord and Sarah Grimké, especially, are striking, for Sarah would also rail against the life of the southern belle, where she "fluttered for a few brief years, my better nature all the while using insurrection against the course I was pursuing, teaching me to despise myself and those who surrounded me in this pageant existence." See Bartlett, ed. *Sarah Grimké*, 115.

26. Angelina E. Grimké, "Appeal to the Christian Women of the South," [1836], reprinted in Ceplair, ed., *The Public Years*, 64.

27. Grimké, "Appeal to the Christian Women," 63–66.

28. This brief description of Louisa McCord's plantation duties has been gleaned from her daughter's unpublished recollections, written in 1900. It clearly attests to the primacy of her mother in her daughter's life, since her father, David McCord, is barely mentioned. It is also apparent that Louisa McCord was indeed in charge of the Lang Syne plantation. See Louisa McCord Smythe, "For Old Lang Syne: Collected for My Children," McCord Family Letters, SCL.

29. Louisa McCord Smythe, "Recollections," McCord Family Letters, SCL. In this collection of memoirs, Mrs. Smythe, Louisa

McCord's daughter, remembers her childhood on the plantation as being "a gentle, patrician life, and one to which we who knew it look back with a longing that is unspeakable."

30. Louisa S. McCord to "Mary" [Mary Cheves?], Oct. 9, 1862, in Dulles-Cheves-McCord-Lovell Papers, South Carolina Historical Society, Charleston, S. C. (hereinafter SCHS). In many of her personal letters, McCord often makes use of the word "stupid" in reference to tasks commonly associated with the feminine. In a much later letter written to her nephew Langdon Cheves, for instance, she writes that "I have been trying to keep very quiet and very stupid, hemming, in good-woman style, pocket handkerchiefs, and so forth." Louisa S. McCord to Langdon Cheves, July 11, 1876, Cheves Papers, SCHS.

31. Louisa S. McCord, *My Dreams* (Philadelphia: Carey and Hart, 1848).

32. Louisa McCord to William Porcher Miles, Dec. 6, 1848, William Porcher Miles Papers, Southern Historical Collection, Wilson Library, University of North Carolina, Chapel Hill, N.C. (hereinafter SHC).

33. Angelina E. Grimké to Theodore Dwight Weld and John Greenleaf Whittier, Aug. 20, 1837, reprinted in Ceplair, ed., *The Public Years*, 281, 283, 284.

34. Angelina E. Grimké, "An Appeal to the Women of the Nominally Free States," [1837], reprinted in Ceplair, ed., *The Public Years*, 132.

35. Angelina E. Grimké, "Letters to Catherine E. Beecher, Letter XII," [1837], reprinted in Ceplair, ed., *The Public Years*, 194.

36. Angelina E. Grimké Weld to Anne Warren Weston, July 15, 1838, reprinted in Ceplair, ed., *The Public Years*, 326.

37. McCord, "Enfranchisement of Woman," 332.

38. Paraphrasing a point made by literary theorist Nina Baym, Susan Harris notes that "female disclaimers of the vote [like the conservative feminist Catharine Beecher] often meant, to those rejecting it, rejection of a sphere of activity associated in the public mind with rudeness, corruption, drunkenness, and *violence*" [emphasis mine]. Harris, *Nineteenth-Century American Women's Novels*, 15.

39. McCord, "Enfranchisement of Woman," 334.

40. When Michael O'Brien included Louisa McCord in his volume *All Clever Men Who Make Their Way* (despite her obvious gender disqualification), he placed her in the masculine political circle within which she hoped to be enscribed. Although she could never take to the stump or hold elected office, Louisa McCord would

have undoubtedly thought it her due to be ranked with such "clever" South Carolinian men as Hugh Legaré and James Henley Thornwell.

41. Louisa S. McCord, "Carey on the Slave Trade," *Southern Quarterly Review* N.S. 9 (Jan., 1854): 115–84 (quotation on p. 168). McCord's formulation of men qua "protectors" of women was a fairly common trope in the mid-nineteenth century and one that was not confined merely to southerners. A female character in a novel by northerner E. D. E. N. Southworth, for example, echoed McCord's sentiments in the following: "Talk of woman's rights; woman's rights live in the instincts of her protector-man." Quoted in Kelley, *Private Woman, Public Stage,* 321.

42. Angelina E. Grimké, "Letters to Catherine E. Beecher, Letter XII," reprinted in Ceplair, ed., *The Public Years,* 197.

43. McCord, "Carey on the Slave Trade," 168–69.

44. Louisa S. McCord, "Woman and Her Needs," *De Bow's Review* 13 (Sept., 1852): 267–90 (quotation on p. 291).

45. Louisa S. McCord, "Charity Which Does Not Begin at Home," *Southern Literary Messenger* 19 (Apr., 1853): 195.

46. McCord, "Woman and Her Needs," 272.

47. McCord, "Enfranchisement of Woman," 343.

48. McCord, "Enfranchisement of Woman," 342, 344.

49. McCord, "Woman and Her Needs," 288. Interestingly enough, it was McCord's notion of sexual difference—of women's primacy in moral matters—that would be used later by early twentieth-century feminists in arguing for the vote as an extension of women's "moral housekeeping." Even later feminist-pacifists adopted this position of essential sexual difference in their claims that women had a distinct moral propensity towards the peaceful resolution of conflict, due mainly to their experience as nurturant mothers.

50. Louisa S. McCord to Augustine T. Smythe, Nov. 14, 1871, Augustine T. Smythe Papers in Smythe/Stoney/Adger Collection, SCHS.

51. Louisa S. McCord to Augustine T. Smythe, March 29, 1874, Smythe Papers, SCHS.

52. Louisa S. McCord, *Caius Gracchus: A Tragedy in Five Acts* (New York: H. Kemot, 1851), 21. In the stanza from which these quotes have been extracted, Cornelia, in obvious self-admonishment, is counseling her ambitious daughter-in-law Licinia. I believe that in these eight lines McCord's private demons are explicated better than in any of her other writings. The full octave reads:

But in our bosoms, if too fierce the flame
That feeds such spirit-struggles, we much check,
Or drive it back, at least, to seeming quiet.
If hard the effort, it is woman's task
Her passions, if not smothered, must be hid,
Till in their faintly beating pulse, herself
Will scarcely know the blood the same which bounds
Through manlier veins unchecked.

53. Louisa S. McCord to William Porcher Miles, Dec. 6, 1848, Miles Papers, SHC.

The Work of Gender in the Southern Renaissance

1. William Faulkner, *Light in August* (New York: Vintage Books, 1990), 449.

2. Faulkner, *Light in August*, 235–36.

3. Sacvan Bercovitch, "The Problem of Ideology in American Literary History," *Critical Inquiry* 12 (Summer, 1986): 635.

4. Kaja Silverman, *Male Subjectivity at the Margins* (New York: Routledge, 1992), 15.

5. Quoted in Peter Filene, *Him/Her/Self: Sex Roles in Modern America*, 2nd ed. (Baltimore: Johns Hopkins University Press, 1986), xiv.

6. Filene, *Him/Her/Self*, 123.

7. Bertram Wyatt-Brown, *Southern Honor: Ethics and Behavior in the Old South* (New York: W. W. Norton and Co., 1982).

8. Lillian Smith, *Killers of the Dream*, rev. ed. (New York: Alfred A. Knopf, 1961), 121.

9. Wilbur J. Cash, *The Mind of the South* (New York, 1941, 1991), 98–9.

The Desperate Imagination

1. Anthony Storr, *Churchill's Black Dog, Kafka's Mice, and Other Phenomena of the Human Mind* (New York: Grove Press, 1988), 265.

2. See Bertram Wyatt-Brown, "The Evolution of Heroes' Honor in the Southern Literary Tradition," in *The Evolution of Southern Culture*, ed. Numan V. Bartley (Athens: University of Georgia Press, 1988), 108–30, and Michael Kreyling, *Figures of the Hero in Southern*

Narrative (Baton Rouge: Louisiana State University Press, 1987); Warwick Wadlington, *Reading Faulknerian Tragedy* (Ithaca: Cornell University Press, 1987).

3. Allen Tate, "The New Provincialism" (1945), in *The Man of Letters: Selected Essays, 1928–1955*, ed. Tate (New York: Meridian Books, 1955, 1960), 330–31. See C. Vann Woodward, "Why the Southern Renaissance?" in *The Future of the Past*, ed. C. Vann Woodward (New York: Oxford University Press, 1989), 203–20.

4. Daniel Singal translated Tate's diagnosis into new terms—the death of Victorianism and the insurgence of a modern sensibility—and reached similar conclusions. Daniel Singal, *The War Within: From Victorian to Modernist Thought in the South, 1919–1945* (Chapel Hill: University of North Carolina Press, 1982).

5. Lewis P. Simpson, *The Dispossessed Garden: Pastoral and History in Southern Literature* (Athens: University of Georgia Press, 1975).

6. Bradford used the phrase in remarks made at a meeting of the St. George Tucker Society, August, 1992, in Atlanta.

7. Phil McCombs, "A Visitor's Interview: Walker Percy," (1987) in *More Conversations with Walker Percy*, eds. Lewis A. Lawson and Victor A. Kramer, (Jackson: University Press of Mississippi, 1993), 187. In recent times the chemistry and neurology of depression have become increasingly clear. The scientific work suggests that sometimes a genetic predisposition plays a role—transmitted from parent to offspring, often more than one, yet randomly striking some descendants but not others. As the seventeenth-century philosopher Robert Burton noted in *The Anatomy of Melancholy*, "I need not therefore make any doubt of Melancholy, but that it is an hereditary disease." The most impressive examples of afflicted lineages include Lord Byron. His wild oscillations of mood could be traced down the corridors of his family's past for one hundred and fifty years. According to psychological studies, about 15 to 20 percent of those of similar disposition belong to clans with notable rates of depressive disorders. See James C. Coyne, ed., *Essential Papers on Depression* (New York: New York University Press, 1985), 1–22, 424; Kay Redfield Jamison, *Touched with Fire: Manic-Depressive Illness and the Artistic Temperament* (New York: Free Press, 1993), 149–90. The range of first-degree relatives of depressives with bipolar symptoms is, according to one study, 5.8 percent to 7.8 percent, much higher than the proportion in the general population. See L. Rifkin and H. Gurling, "Genetic

Aspects of Affective Disorders," in *Biological Aspects of Affective Disorders*, eds. R. Horton and C. Katona (London: Academic Press, 1991), 305–34.

8. Quotation, Louis D. Rubin, Jr., *The Mocking Bird in the Gum Tree: A Literary Gallimaufry* (Baton Rouge: Louisiana State University, 1991), 77.

9. Cf. Tom Dardis, *The Thirsty Muse: Alcohol and the American Writer* (New York: Ticknor and Fields, 1989) claims that alcoholism is a disease affecting the normal and disturbed personality with equal virulence. For a more informed view of how alcohol and depression are related, see Frederick K. Goodwin and Kay Redfield Jamison, *Manic-Depressive Illness* (New York: Oxford University Press, 1990), 210, also 211–26, and Francis Mark Mondimore, *Depression: The Mood Disease* (Baltimore: Johns Hopkins University Press, 1990), 156–63; also the confessions of William Styron, *Darkness Visible: A Memoir of Madness* (New York: Random House: 1990), 40–50.

10. Kathleen Woodward, "Late Theory, Late Style: Loss and Renewal in Freud and Barthes," in *Aging and Gender in Literature: Studies in Creativity*, in eds. Anne Wyatt-Brown and Janice Rossen (Charlottesville: University Press of Virginia, 1993), 82.

11. Phyllis Greenacre, "The Family Romance of the Artist," *The Psychoanalytic Study of the Child* (New York: International Universities Press, 1958), 13: 9–36; George H. Pollock, "The Mourning Process, the Creative Process, and the Creation," in *The Problem of Loss and Mourning: Psychoanalytic Perspectives*, eds. David R. Dietrich and Peter C. Shabad (Madison, Conn.: International Universities Press, Inc., 1989), 27–59; George H. Pollock, "Anniversary Reactions, Trauma, and Mourning," *Psychoanalytic Quarterly* 39 (July, 1970): 347–71.

12. William Styron, "Why Primo Levi Need Not Have Died," *New York Times*, December 19, 1988, National edition, p. 23.

13. Rubin, *The Mockingbird*, 51.

14. Peter Mathiessen and George Plimpton, "The Art of Fiction V: William Styron," (1954), in *Conversations with William Styron*, ed. James L. W. West III (Jackson: University Press of Mississippi, 1985), 19.

15. Quoted in Virginia Spencer Carr, *The Lonely Hunter: A Biography of Carson McCullers* (New York: Doubleday, 1975), 2, see also 290ff.

16. Marianne M. Moates, *A Bridge of Childhood: Truman Capote's Southern Years* (New York: Henry Holt, 1989), 1–50; Bertram

Wyatt-Brown, *The House of Percy: Honor, Melancholy, and Imagination in a Southern Family* (New York: Oxford University Press, 1994); Jay Tolson, *Pilgrim in the Ruins: A Life of Walker Percy* (New York: Simon and Schuster, 1992).

17. John Malcolm Brinnin, *Truman Capote: Dear Heart, Old Buddy* (New York: Delacorte, 1981, 1986), 13.

18. Dotson Rader, "The Art of Theatre V: Tennessee Williams," in *Conversations with Tennessee Williams*, ed. Albert J. Devlin (Jackson, Miss.: University Press of Mississippi, 1986), 327, 360 (quotation); Tennessee Williams, *Memoirs* (New York: Doubleday, 1972), 116–29; Dakin Williams and Shepherd Mead, *Tennessee Williams: An Intimate Biography* (New York: Arbor House, 1983); Donald Spoto, *The Kindness of Strangers: The Life of Tennessee Williams* (New York: Ballantine, 1985). On Glasgow, see Anne Goodwyn Jones, *Tomorrow Is Another Day: The Woman Writer in the South, 1859–1936* (Baton Rouge: Louisiana State University Press, 1981), 228.

19. William Styron, *A Tidewater Morning: Three Tales from Youth* (New York: Random House, 1993), 28 (quotation).

20. D. A. Callard, *Pretty Good for a Woman: The Enigmas of Evelyn Scott* (New York: W. W. Norton, 1985), 2–3, 6 (quotation); Robert Louis Welker, "Evelyn Scott; A Literary Biography" (Ph.D. diss., Vanderbilt University, 1958), 54.

21. Joan Givner, *Katherine Anne Porter: A Life* (New York: Simon and Schuster, 1982), 35–43, 43 (quotation).

22. Givner, *Katherine Anne Porter: A Life*, 516–17 n. 14.

23. Givner, *Katherine Anne Porter: A Life*, 54. Cluetts Machann and William Bedford Clark, eds., *Katherine Anne Porter and Texas: An Uneasy Relationship* (College Station: Texas A&M University Press, 1990). One is reminded of the upbringing of Rudyard Kipling, who, along with his sister, was abandoned by parents, off to India, leaving their children to board with a sadistic couple on the English moors. See Rudyard Kipling, *The Light That Failed* (Boston: Ticknor and Fields, 1898).

24. David Herbert Donald, *Look Homeward: A Life of Thomas Wolfe* (Boston: Little, Brown, 1987), 1–11 passim.

25. LeRoy Percy to Mrs. C. J. McKinney, January 25, 1926, Percy Family Papers and entry for April 3, 1932, Henry Waring Ball Diary, both collections, in the Mississippi Department of Archives and History, Jackson; Tolson, *Pilgrim in the Ruins*, 42, 44–45, 98; Greenville *Delta Democrat-Times*, April 2, 1932.

26. Edward Butscher, *Conrad Aiken: Poet of White Horse Vale* (Athens: University of Georgia Press, 1988), 21.

27. Butscher, *Aiken*, 44–46, 48 (quotation), 52–53.

28. About the house in Little Rock Fletcher wrote, "The house with its many memories watched from behind the great wall,/The carven and paneled doorway, the green wood shutters so tall,/ That my mother always kept closed through the night for she was afraid." In "Towards the North Star," in John Gould Fletcher, *Selected Poems of John Gould Fletcher* (Fayetteville: University of Arkansas Press, 1988), 303.

29. Ben Johnson, "John Gould Fletcher," 29–30, manuscript in press, kindly lent by the author.

30. Carr, *The Lonely Hunter*, 302 (quotation), 26–28, 298–302; Anthony Storr, *The Dynamics of Creation* (New York: Atheneum, 1972), 79; John Bowlby, *Attachment and Loss, Volume II, Separation: Anxiety and Anger* (New York: Basic Books, 1973), 309–12.

31. Michael Ignatieff, "Paradigm Lost," *Times Literary Supplement*, Sept. 4, 1987, 939.

32. William Faulkner, *Intruder in the Dust* (New York: Modern Library, 1948), 194 (quotation).

33. Douglas Barzelay and Robert Sussman, "William Styron on *The Confessions of Nat Turner:* A *Yale Lit* Interview," (1968), in *Conversations with William Styron*, ed. West, 105.

34. Fred Hobson, *The Southern Writer in the Postmodern World* (Athens: University of Georgia Press, 1991), 2.

35. Joel Williamson, *William Faulkner and Southern History* (New York: Oxford University Press, 1993), 384.

36. Edgar Allan Poe to George Eveleth, January 4, 1848, in *The Letters of Edgar Allan Poe*, ed. John Wand Ostram, 2 vols. (Cambridge: Harvard University Press, 1948), 2:356.

37. Kenneth Silverman, *Edgar A. Poe: Mournful and Never-Ending Remembrance* (New York: HarperCollins, 1991), 373–74.

38. Simpson, *The Dispossessed Garden*, 68–69.

39. On Tucker, see Drew Gilpin Faust, *A Sacred Circle: The Dilemma of the Intellectual in the Old South, 1840–1860* (Baltimore: Johns Hopkins University Press, 1977), 20–27; Robert J. Brugger, *Beverley Tucker: Heart over Head in the Old South* (Baltimore: Johns Hopkins University Press, 1978). Tucker was much affected by the tragic deaths in his family early in his life; he lost his mother and a succession of brothers and sisters in the 1790s (p. 11). On Lincoln's depression and poetry writing, see Howard I. Kushner, *Self-*

Destruction in the Promised Land: A Psychocultural Biology of American Suicide (New Brunswick: Rutgers University Press, 1989), 132–44; On Timrod, see Louis D. Rubin, Jr., *The Edge of the Swamp: A Study in the Literature and Society of the Old South* (Baton Rouge: Louisiana State University, 1989), 190–225.

40. See, for a sensitive reading of such documents, Michael O'Brien, introduction to *An Evening When Alone: Four Journals of Single Women in the South, 1827–67*, ed. Michael O'Brien (Charlottesville: University Press of Virginia, 1993), 1–49. Thomas quoted in Virginia Ingraham Burr, ed., *The Secret Eye: The Journal of Ella Gertrude Clanton Thomas, 1848–1889* (Chapel Hill: University of North Carolina Press, 1990), 305. See also Charles East, introduction to *The Civil War Diary of Sarah Morgan*, ed. Charles East (Athens: University of Georgia Press, 1991), xv–xli; Charles A. Le Guin, ed., *A Home-Concealed Woman: The Diaries of Magnolia Wynn Le Guin, 1901–1913* (Athens: University of Georgia Press, 1990).

41. James Henry Hammond, *Secret and Sacred: The Diaries of James Henry Hammond, A Southern Slaveholder*, ed. Carol Bleser (New York: Oxford University Press, 1988).

42. Faust, *Sacred Circle*; Faust uncovers the connection between psychological problems and the alienation of this group of intellectuals, but she stresses social more than personal factors in their cries of self-pity and mutual defensiveness against a society that they believed did not appreciate their virtuosity.

43. See Hobson, *Tell about the South*, 44–63.

44. Edmund Ruffin, *Incidents of My Life: Edmund Ruffin's Autobiographical Essays*, ed. David F. Allmendinger (Charlottesville: University Press of Virginia, 1990), Appendix 2, 184–85; see also David F. Allmendinger, Jr., *Ruffin: Family and Reform in the Old South* (New York: Oxford University Press, 1990); David F. Allmendinger, Jr., "The Early Career of Edmund Ruffin, 1810–1840," *Virginia Magazine of History and Biography* 93 (1985): 127–54; William Kauffman Scarborough, introduction to *The Diary of Edmund Ruffin*, ed. William Kauffman Scarborough, 3 vols. (Baton Rouge: Louisiana State University Press, 1972–89), 1: xv–lxv; Robert J. Brugger, *Beverley Tucker: Head over Heart in the Old South* (Baltimore: Johns Hopkins University Press, 1978).

45. Quotation, entry for March 11, 1861, in C. Vann Woodward, ed., *Mary Chesnut's Civil War* (New Haven: Yale University Press, 1981), 23. Michael O'Brien, "Mary Chesnut," Southern Intellectual History Circle meeting, February, 1994.

46. Emily Toth, *Kate Chopin* (1990; Austin: University of Texas Press, 1993), 336–52.

47. Williamson, *Faulkner and Southern History*, 238–39 (from James B. Meriwether, "Faulkner Lost and Found," *New York Times Book Review*, November 5, 1972, 7.)

48. On Balzac, see Storr, *Dynamics of Creation*, 85; Leon Edel, *Henry James: A Life* (New York: Random House, 1985), 425–47. Taylor is quoted in Barbara Thompson, "Interview with Peter Taylor" (1987), in *Conversations with Peter Taylor*, ed. Hubert H. McAlexander (Jackson: University Press of Mississippi, 1987), 154.

49. John Batchelor, *The Life of Joseph Conrad* (Oxford, Eng.: Blackwell's, 1994), 59–60; Carr, *The Lonely Hunter*, 32.

50. See Jamison, *Touched with Fire*, 60; Paul Delany, *D. H. Lawrence's Nightmare: The Writer and His Circle in the Years of the Great War* (New York: Basic Books, 1978), 187–89; A. Alvarez, *The Savage God: A Study of Suicide* (New York: Random House, 1972), 128; Jay Martin, *Who Am I This Time? Uncovering the Fictive Personality* (New York: W. W. Norton, 1988), 172–78. Only a few of the literary connections can be stated here. Gustave Flaubert had considerable influence on Truman Capote, see Brinnin, *Truman Capote*, 6, 19, 149; Faulkner, Frederick R. Karl, *William Faulkner: American Writer, A Biography* (New York: Ballantine Books, 1989), 89; on William Styron along with James Joyce, James L. West, Jr., ed., *Conversations with William Styron* (Jackson: University Press of Mississippi, 1985), 12. Walker Percy acknowledged many times his indebtedness to Dostoyevsky, as well as Albert Camus and Jean-Paul Sartre. See William Rodney Allen, *Walker Percy: A Southern Wayfarer* (Jackson: University Press of Mississippi, 1986), 5, 19, 21, 23, 25, 91, 107, 155.

51. "How can I not connect *The Brothers Karamazov* with the big fat Random House edition, fat as a Bible, its pages slightly pulpy, crumbling at the corners and smelling like bread?" Walker Percy recollected. "And how can I disconnect Ivan and Mitya from reading about them sitting in a swing on my grandmother's porch in Athens, Georgia, in the 1930s?" Harriet Doar, interview, 1962, in Lewis A. Lawson and Victor A. Kramer, eds., *Conversations with Walker Percy* (Jackson: University Press of Mississippi, 1985), 5; quotation from Walker Percy, introduction to *Walker Percy: A Comprehensive Descriptive Bibliography*, by Linda Whitney Hobson (New Orleans: Faust Publishing Co., 1988), xviii. See also Robert Coles, *Walker Percy: An American Search* (Boston: Little, Brown, 1978), 72. Jo-

seph Frank, *Dostoevsky: The Seeds of Revolt, 1821–49* (Princeton: Princeton University Press, 1976), 6–41.

52. McCullers quoted in Carr, *The Lonely Hunter*, 32. Lewis A. Lawson, "Walker Percy's Indirect Communications," in Lewis A. Lawson, *Following Percy: Essays on Walker's Work* (Troy, N. Y.: Whitston Publishing Co., 1988), 26; Lawson and Kramer, eds., *Conversations with Walker Percy*, 3, 5, 10, 12, 14, 18, 31, 66, 75, 259–60, 298.

53. See Wyatt-Brown, "The Evolution of Heroes' Honor," 108–30.

54. Quoted in Tennessee Williams, *Memoirs*, 85; Storr, *The Dynamics of Creation*, 79 (quotation).

55. Sigmund Freud, "A Special Type of Choice of Object Made by Men (Contributions to the Psychology of Love I)," in *The Complete Psychological Works of Sigmund Freud*, trans. James Strachey, 24 vols. (London: Hogarth, 1951), 11: 165.

56. See especially, Donald, *Look Homeward*, 213–19, 215 (quotation), 401.

57. Joseph Blotner, *Faulkner: A Biography*, 2 vols. (New York: Random House, 1974), 1:687; Carr, *The Lonely Hunter*, 90–91.

58. C. Hugh Holman and Sue Fields Ross, eds., *The Letters of Thomas Wolfe to His Mother* (Chapel Hill: University of North Carolina Press, 1968), 119.

59. Williamson, *Faulkner*, 207; Blotner, *Faulkner*, 1: 488; William Faulkner, "Divorce in Naples," in *Collected Stories of William Faulkner*, ed. Joseph Blotner (New York: Random House, 1950, 1976), 877–94.

60. See Richard H. King, *A Southern Renaissance: The Cultural Awakening of the American South, 1930–1955* (New York: Oxford University Press, 1980), 85–98, esp. 96–97.

61. Nonetheless, Percy had his friends Maxwell Perkins and Ford Maddox Ford read Erwin's manuscript. William Alexander Percy to John Seymour Erwin, September, [1941?], and two other letters, both n.d., 1940, in possession of John Seymour Erwin, Sun City Center, Florida, copies kindly lent to the author.

62. Gerald Clarke, *Capote: A Biography* (New York: Simon and Schuster, 1988), 161–62.

63. See Peggy W. Prenshaw's sensitive reading, "The Paradoxical Southern World of Tennessee Williams," in *Tennessee Williams: A Tribute*, ed. Jac Tharpe (Jackson: University Press of Mississippi, 1977), 3–29; Rader, "The Art of Theatre V: Tennessee Williams," 344; Spoto, *Kindness of Strangers*, 245–46.

64. Quoted in Laurence Bergreen, *James Agee: A Life* (New York: Penguin, 1984, 1985), 239; see also 3–19, 124–25, 144.

65. Rubin, *The Mockingbird in the Gum Tree*, 44 (quotation), 46, 48.

66. Hobson, *Tell about the South*, 8.

67. Williams, *Memoirs*, 139.

68. Cf. Michael Millgate, *The Achievement of William Faulkner* (1963; Athens: University of Georgia Press, 1989), 30–34; Henry James quoted in Edel, *Henry James*, 429.

69. Gail Godwin, *A Southern Family* (New York: Avon, 1987), 218.

70. Williams, *Memoirs*, 144.

71. Quoted in Donald, *Look Homeward*, 189; second quotation from Thomas Wolfe to Aline Bernstein, November 9, 1926, in *My Other Loneliness: Letters of Thomas Wolfe and Aline Bernstein*, ed. Suzanne Stutman (Chapel Hill: University of North Carolina Press, 1983), 117.

72. Donald, *Look Homeward*, 461–63.

73. Clarke, *Capote*, 536–47.

74. See King, *A Southern Renaissance*, 139–45; Frederick R. Karl, *William Faulkner: American Writer* (New York: Ballantine, 1989), 11–26.

75. William Faulkner's sexual initiation, despite years visiting cathouses with his friend Phil Stone, did not occur as early as his posture of swaggering bravado suggested. Williamson, *Faulkner*, 187, 204, 213–16.

76. Faulkner quoted in Martin, *Who Am I This Time?*, 189; Williamson, *Faulkner and Southern History*, 184 (Sally Murry quotation), 185, 250; Tom Dardis, *The Thirsty Muse: Alcohol and the American Writer* (New York: Ticknor and Fields, 1989), 27.

77. Williamson, *William Faulkner and Southern History*, 249.

78. See Dardis, *The Thirsty Muse*, 25–95, esp. 33–34.

79. Styron, *Darkness Visible*, 40.

80. Quoted in Johnson, "Fletcher, " 315.

81. Randall Jarrell, "90 North," in *Randall Jarrell: The Complete Poems* (New York: Farrar, Straus, and Giroux, 1969), 113–14 (quotation, lines 29–33); William H. Pritchard, *Randall Jarrell: A Literary Life* (New York: Farrar, Straus, and Giroux, 1990), 290–95. Styron, *Darkness Visible*, 32: "Randall Jarrell almost certainly killed himself. He did so not because he was a coward, nor out of any moral feebleness, but because he was afflicted with a depression that was so devas-

tating that he could no longer endure the pain of it." On Cash, see Bertram Wyatt-Brown, "Introduction: The Mind of W. J. Cash," in W. J. Cash, *The Mind of the South* (New York: Random House, 1991), vii–xliv; idem, "Creativity and Suffering in a Southern Writer: W. J. Cash," *W. J. Cash and the Minds of the South,* ed. Paul Escott (Baton Rouge: Louisiana State University Press, 1992), 38–66; Bruce Clayton, *W. J. Cash: A Life* (Baton Rouge: Louisiana State University Press, 1991). On Cason see Wayne Flynt, introduction to *90° in the Shade,* by Clarence Cason (University: University of Alabama Press, 1935, 1989), v–x.

82. Leslie Stephen, "Charlotte Brontë," in idem, *Hours in the Library,* 3 vols. (London and New York, Johnson Reprint Co., 1832, 1968), 3: 10.

83. J. William Broadway, "A Conversation with Peter Taylor" (1985), in McAlexander, ed., *Conversations with Peter Taylor,* 111.

84. Quoted, Carr, *The Lonely Hunter,* 298.

85. Freud quoted in Storr, *Churchill's Black Dog,* 159.

86. Faulkner, *Intruder in the Dust,* 194.

Styron's Choice

1. Petersburg, Virginia, *Intelligencer* quoted in Richmond *Enquirer,* November 22, 1831. Thomas Gray's interviews with Nat Turner, the key source for practically everyone who has written on the subject, are published as Thomas R. Gray, *The Confessions of Nat Turner, the Leader of the Late Insurrection in Southampton County, Va., As Fully and Voluntarily Made to Thomas R. Gray, in the Prison Where He was Confined, and Acknowledged by Him To Be Such When Read before the Court of Southampton . . .* (Richmond: Thomas R. Gray, 1831). Gray's *Confessions* have been widely reprinted, including in John Henrik Clarke, ed., *William Styron's Nat Turner: Ten Black Writers Respond* (Boston: Beacon Press, 1968), 93–118; Henry Irving Tragle, ed., *The Southampton Slave Revolt of 1831: A Compilation of Source Material including the Full Text of the Confessions of Nat Turner* (Amherst, Mass.: University of Massachusetts Press, 1971, rpt. New York, 1973), 300–321, and in John B. Duff and Peter M. Mitchell, eds., *The Nat Turner Rebellion: The Historical Event and the Modern Controversy* (New York: Harper and Row, 1971), 11–30. See also Thomas Wentworth Higginson, "Nat Turner's Insurrection," *Atlantic Monthly,* 8 (Aug., 1861), reprinted in his *Travellers and Outlaws* (Boston: Lee and Shepard, 1889), reprinted as *Black Rebellion* (New York: Arno Press, 1969), 207; William Sidney

Drewry, *The Southampton Insurrection* (Washington, 1900), 98–102;
John W. Cromwell, "The Aftermath of Nat Turner's Insurrection,"
Journal of Negro History 5 (1920), 212–34.

2. C. Vann Woodward was the first, I believe, to call attention
to Nat Turner as "a kind of Christ-figure. Consider his age, his trade
as a carpenter, his march on Jerusalem, his martyrdom." See C. Vann
Woodward and R. W. B. Lewis, "The Confessions of William Styron,"
an interview with William Styron on November 5, 1967, in *Conversations with William Styron*, ed. James L. W. West, III (Jackson:
University Press of Mississippi, 1985), 88 (hereinafter cited as *Conversations*) and C. Vann Woodward, "Confessions of a Rebel: 1831,"
New Republic, Oct. 7, 1967, 26. Throughout Styron's oeuvre essential
humanity depends on an *imitation Christi*, according to John Douglas Lang, "William Styron: The Christian Imagination" (Ph.D. diss.,
Stanford University, 1975). Styron, however, constructed his Nat
Turner as "an avenging Old Testament angel" and explicitly es-
chewed Christian parallels. "I avoided mention of Christ as much as
I could throughout the book," he said. "I really saw Nat as a man
profoundly motivated by the empathy he feels with the old prophets,
Ezekial, Jeremiah, Isaiah."

3. James Jones and William Styron, "Two Writers Talk It Over,"
Esquire 60 (July, 1963), 58, reprinted in *Conversations*, 43; Phyllis
Meras, "Phyllis Meras Interviews William Styron," *Saturday Review*
(Oct. 7, 1967), 30.

4. Benna Kay Kime emphasizes the sheer technical virtuosity of
Styron's narrative techniques in "A Critical Study of the Technique of
William Styron" (Ph.D. diss., Tulane University, 1971).

5. Meras, "Interviews William Styron," 30. According to Henry
Grady Morgan, Jr., Styron's novels all represent the world as a prison
and imprisonment as the human condition from which there is no
escape. See his "The World as a Prison: A Study of the Novels of William Styron" (Ph.D. diss., University of Colorado, 1973). Sandra M.
Peterson sees Turner's testimony to Gray in Styron's *Confessions* as
part of a continuum from Puritan confessional literature through *The
Scarlet Letter, Billy Budd*, and *An American Tragedy* in her "The
View from the Gallows: The Criminal Confession in American Literature" (Ph.D. diss., Northwestern University, 1972). W. A. Kort
explores connections between what he called "the resources of confessional fiction" and "the phenomenon of a revolutionary act" in
"*The Confessions of Nat Turner* and the Dynamic Revolution," in

Shriven Selves: Religious Problems in Recent American Fiction
(Philadelphia: Fortress Press, 1972), 116–40.

6. Styron, *The Confessions of Nat Turner* (New York: Random House, 1966), 35. Hereinafter cited in the text within parentheses as *CONT*.

7. *CONT*, 132.

8. *CONT*, 123, 135, 169.

9. *CONT*, 232.

10. *CONT*, 127–98, 169–98.

11. *CONT*, 156–57, 191.

12. *CONT*, 211ff.

13. *CONT*, 287.

14. *CONT*, 157.

15. *CONT*, 258–59, 279–80.

16. *CONT*, 259–60.

17. *CONT*, 260.

18. *CONT*, 55–56.

19. *CONT*, 250.

20. *CONT*, 366–71, 381–94, 48, 109, 348.

21. *CONT*, 371–81, 95, 92, 91.

22. *CONT*, 401–402.

23. *CONT*, 403.

24. Meras, "Interviews with William Styron," 30.

25. Meras, "Interviews with William Styron," 30.

26. C. Vann Woodward, "Clio with Soul," *American Historical Review* 75 (1970), 712. One interesting early review was that of Philip Rahv in the *New York Review of Books*. "I think that only a white Southern writer could have brought it off," Rahv gushed. A Northerner would have been too much 'outside' the experience to manage it effectively." Then he added that "a Negro writer, because of a very complex anxiety not only personal but social and political, would have probably stacked the cards, producing a mood of unnerving rage and indignation, a melodrama of saints and sinners." Rahv's comments were not only patronizing; they were prophetic of the rage and indignation to follow. See his "Through the Midst of Jerusalem," *New York Review of Books*, Oct. 26, 1967, 6–10.

27. See, for example, Herbert Aptheker, "A Note on the History," *The Nation*, Oct. 16, 1967, 375–76; Herbert Aptheker and William Styron, "Truth and Nat Turner: An Exchange," *The Nation*, Apr. 22, 1968, 543–47; and Vincent Harding and Eugene D. Genovese, "An Ex-

change on Nat Turner," *New York Review of Books*, Nov. 7, 1968, 35–37. Richard Gilman was one of the few critics who ventured a dissenting literary judgment: "Nat Turner seems to me a mediocre novel," he wrote, "not a beautiful or even well-written work of fiction which happens to contain historical inaccuracies or perversions of historical truth." See his "Nat Turner Revisited," *The New Republic*, Apr. 27, 1968, 23–32. In his *The Return of Nat Turner: History, Literature, and Cultural Politics in Sixties America* (Athens: University of Georgia Press, 1992), Albert E. Stone summarizes the controversy and echoes the criticism with uncritical approval, adding to it his own prosecution of the author as a manipulative opportunist in pursuit of fame and fortune.

28. Albert Murray, "A Troublesome Property," *The New Leader*, Dec. 4, 1967, 18–21; *William Styron's Nat Turner: Ten Black Writers Respond* ed. John Henrik Clarke (Boston: Beacon Press, 1968), hereinafter *TBWR*.

29. Alvin Poussaint, "*The Confessions of Nat Turner* and the Dilemma of William Styron," *TBWR*, 21; Ernest Kaiser, "The Failure of William Styron," *TBWR*, 63; Vincent Harding, "You've Taken My Nat and Gone," *TBWR*, 29, 20; John Oliver Killens, "The Confessions of Willie Styron," *TBWR*, 43–44; Lerone Bennett, Jr., "Nat's Last White Man," *TBWR*, 5.

30. Harding, "You've Taken My Nat and Gone," *TBWR*, 26. Styron departs here from his principal primary source, Gray's *Confessions*. See Gray, *Confessions*, in *TBWR*, 100.

31. Bennett, "Nat's Last White Man," *TBWR*, 8–9; Gray's*Confessions* have been widely reprinted, most notably as an appendix to *TBWR*, 99–100; *CONT*, 132. See also F. Roy Johnson, *The Nat Turner Slave Insurrection* (Murfreesboro, N.C.: Johnson Publishing Co., 1966), 228–30.

32. Kaiser, "Failure of William Styron," *TBWR*, 56; Gray, "Confessions," in *TBWR*, 99, 102; Johnson, *Nat Turner Insurrection*, 232–33. As early as 1965 Styron had expressed his enthusiasm for what he called Erikson's "brilliant study of the development of the revolutionary impulse in a young man, and the relationship of this impulse to the father figure." It apparently led him to surmise that "Nat Turner's relationship with his father (or his surrogate father, his master) was tormented and complicated, like Luther's." See William Styron, *This Quiet Dust and Other Writings* (New York: Random House, 1982), 16.

33. Poussaint, "Dilemma of William Styron," *TBWR*, 18–19; Bennett, "Nat's Last White Man," *TBWR*, 9.

34. John A. Williams, "The Manipulation of History and of Fact: An Ex-Southerner's Apologist Tract for Slavery and the Life of Nat Turner; or, William Styron's Faked Confessions," *TBWR*, 48; Killens, "Confessions of Willie Styron," *TBWR*, 36–37.

35. Poussaint, "Dilemma of William Styron," *TBWR*, 21; Killens, "Confessions of Willie Styron," *TBWR*, 40; Bennett, "Nat's Last White Man," *TBWR*, 11, 6. The main charges are summarized in Eugene D. Genovese's spirited defense of Styron, "The Nat Turner Case," *New York Review of Books*, Sept. 12, 1968, 34–37; reprinted as "William Styron before the People's Court" in his *In Red and Black: Marxian Explorations in Southern and Afro-American History*, 2nd ed. (Knoxville: University of Tennessee Press, 1984), 204, 210. But see also James M. McPherson, preface to Thomas Wentworth Higginson, *Black Rebellion* (New York, 1969), xi; and Johnson, *Nat Turner Insurrection*, 239.

36. Harding, "You've Taken My Nat and Gone," *TBWR*, 28; Bennett, "Nat's Last White Man," *TBWR*, 13; Mike Thelwell, "Back With the Wind: Mr. Styron and the Reverend Turner," *TBWR*, 88–89, *CONT*, 107–108, 370, 390.

37. Bennett, "Nat's Last White Man," *TBWR*, 13–15; Gray, *Confessions* in *TBWR*, 107–108.

38. Bennett, "Nat's Last White Man," *TBWR*, 15; Loyle Hairston, "William Styron's Nat Turner—Rogue-Nigger," *TBWR*, 67.

39. Kaiser, "Failure of William Styron," *TBWR*, 63; Harding, "You've Taken My Nat and Gone, " *TBWR*, 29.

40. Bennett, "Nat's Last White Man," *TBWR*, 4; Kaiser, "Failure of William Styron," *TBWR*, 64; Poussaint, "Dilemma of William Styron," *TBWR*, 21.

41. Styron's pre-*Confessions* attitude toward critics is indicated in an interview with Madeleine Chapsal in *L'Express*, Mar. 8, 1962, 26–27, reprinted as "Interview," in *Conversations*, 23–24. The text of the Southern Historical Association panel discussion is reprinted as Ralph Ellison, William Styron, Robert Penn Warren, and C. Vann Woodward, "The Uses of History in Fiction" in *Conversations*, but the words alone hardly recapture the ambience of the experience. Styron's exchange with his critic is on p. 122. Ellison declared of Styron, "One thing that I know is that he isn't a bigot, he isn't a racist." And Woodward declared that Styron in the *Confessions* "comes

very close, indeed, given the license of the novelist, to doing what the historian does in reconstructing the past." See "The Uses of History in Fiction," 116, 131.

42. Styron, author's note in *Confessions,* vii; Styron, introduction to *This Quiet Dust,* 4; Barzelay and Sussman, "William Styron," 24–25, reprinted in *Conversations,* 95; James L. W. West III, "A Bibliographer's Interview with William Styron," *Costerus,* N. S. 4 (1975), 13–29, reprinted in *Conversations,* 209.

43. Barzelay and Sussman, "William Styron," 94; Robert Canzoneri and Page Stegner, "An Interview with William Styron," in *Conversations,* 67–68; Bertram Wyatt-Brown, review of Stone's *Return of Nat Turner,* in *Journal of Southern History* 59 (1993), 587. Styron had earlier said that he intended the "meditation on history" tag "to take the curse of the label 'historical novel' off the book, because it has regrettably acquired a pejorative connotation." See Woodward and Lewis, "Confessions of William Styron," 86. Robert Penn Warren, writing on the same subject, notes in the foreword to the revised edition of his *Brother to Dragons,* that "a poem dealing with history is no more at liberty to violate what the writer takes to be the spirit of history than it is at liberty to violate what he takes to be the nature of the human heart." See Robert Penn Warren, *Brother to Dragons,* rev. ed. (New York: Random House, 1979), quoted in C. Vann Woodward, *The Future of the Past* (New York: Oxford University Press, 1989), 233.

44. Eugene D. Genovese, "The Nat Turner Case," *New York Review of Books,* Sept. 12, 1968, 34–37; reprinted as "William Styron before the People's Court," in his *In Red and Black,* 200–217. Pagination is to "William Styron before the People's Court." The quote is on p. 202.

45. Genovese, "William Styron before the People's Court," 203–204; "William Styron on *The Confessions of Nat Turner,*" 100; William W. Freehling, *The Road to Disunion: Secessionists at Bay, 1776–1854* (New York: Oxford University Press, 1990), 180–81. Nat had told Gray that the young slaves looked up to him and chose him as their leader because of his ability to read. See Gray, "Confessions," in *TBWR,* 100–101. See also Johnson, *Nat Turner Insurrection,* 231. The contemporary press did not hesitate to convict Nat Turner of cowardice. According to the *Richmond Enquirer,* the rebel leader "acknowledges himself a coward, and says, he was actuated to do what he did, from the influence of fanaticism." After his capture, the paper noted, he had become "convinced that he has done wrong, and ad-

vises all other Negroes not to follow his example." See the *Richmond Enquirer,* Nov. 8, 1831, in Duff and Mitchell, eds., *Nat Turner Rebellion,* 37. On Thomas Gray, see the new revelations in Thomas C. Parramore, *Southampton County, Virginia* (Charlottesville: University Press of Virginia, 1978).

46. Genovese, "William Styron before the People's Court," 206–207; David Walker, *Appeal in Four Articles, Together with a Preamble to the Coloured Citizens in the World, but in Particular, and Very Expressly, to those of the United States of America* (1829–1830), quoted in Genovese, *In Red and Black,* 207.

47. Killens, "Confessions of Willie Styron," *TBWR,* 41; John Floyd, governor of Virginia, to James Hamilton, Jr., governor of South Carolina, Nov. 19, 1831, in Duff and Mitchell, eds., *Nat Turner Rebellion,* 43.

48. To say that the Elkins thesis proved controversial is to understate. His concentration camp analogy drew fire from the right while his Sambo characterization drew fire from the left. Elkins acknowledged that the system worked less efficiently in practice than in theory. "It was possible for significant numbers, of slaves, in varying degrees, to escape the full impact of the system and its coercions upon personality," he wrote. "For all such people there was a margin of space denied to the majority; the system's authority-structure claimed their bodies but not quite their souls." Nevertheless, he insisted that harsh systems have harsh effects. See Stanley M. Elkins, *Slavery: A Problem in American Institutonal and Intellectual Life* (Chicago: University of Chicago Press, 1959), 86. For examples of the response to Elkins, see Ann J. Lane, ed., *The Debate over Slavery* (Urbana: University of Illinois Press, 1971).

49. Stanley M. Elkins, *Slavery: A Problem in American Institutional and Intellectual Life,* 2nd ed. (Chicago: University of Chicago Press, 1963), ix, 81–89; Ulrich B. Phillips, *American Negro Slavery* (New York: D. Appleton, 1918); and his *Life and Labor in the Old South* (Boston: Little, Brown, 1929), quotation on 217.

50. Bennett, "Nat's Last White Man," *TBWR,* 7, 4; Ernest Kaiser, "The Failure of William Styron," *TBWR,* 50–65; Williams, "Manipulation of History," *TBWR,* 45–49; and Killens, "The Confessions of Willie Styron," *TBWR,* 34–44.

51. William Styron, "Truth and Nat Turner: An Exchange," *The Nation,* Apr. 22, 1968, 545; Eugene D. Genovese, "The Nat Turner Case," *New York Review of Books,* Sept. 12, 1968, 34–37; Barzelay and Sussman, "William Styron," 106.

52. Higginson, "Nat Turner's Insurrection," 169; Barzelay and Sussman, "William Styron," 106; Howard Meyer, *Colonel of the Black Regiment: The Life of Thomas Wentworth Higginson* (New York: W. W. Norton, 1967), 156.

53. William Sidney Drewry, *The Southampton Slave Insurrection* (Washington: Neale Co., 1900), also published as *Slave Insurrection in Virginia, 1830–1865*; Canzoneri and Stegner, "Interview with William Styron," 68. There were more recent secondary sources as well. Herbert Aptheker, for instance, maintained that another of Nat Turner's sons, Gilbert, had become a respected citizen of Zanesville, Ohio, and had died there a decade before Styron was born. And Lucy Mae Turner, who claimed to be Nat Turner's granddaughter, had published an article on the Turner family in 1955. See also Herbert Aptheker, "Truth and Nat Turner: An Exchange," *The Nation,* Apr. 22, 1968, 543. Interestingly enough, Aptheker rejects Drewry's book as "untruthful" on most questions, but believes Drewry's report of Nat's wife and son. See also Lucy Mae Turner, "The Family of Nat Turner," *Negro History Bulletin,* 18 (Mar., 1955), 127–32; and Stephen B. Oates, *Fires of Jubilee: Nat Turner's Fierce Rebellion* (New York: Harper and Row, 1975), 32.

54. Unsigned communication to *Richmond Whig,* Sept. 17, 1831, in Duff and Mitchell, eds., *Nat Turner Rebelion,* 35. Genovese revised his sentence in the second edition of his collection of essays, *In Red and Black,* to read, "The evidence for Turner's alleged black wife is slim and not beyond challenge." See Genovese, "William Styron before the People's Court," 210.

55. William Styron, "Truth and Nat Turner: An Exchange," *The Nation,* Apr. 22, 1968, 547; Woodward and Lewis, "Confessions of William Styron," 90.

56. Gray, "Confessions," in *TBWR,* 105.

57. Winthrop D. Jordan, *Tumult and Silence at Second Creek: An Inquiry into a Civil War Slave Conspiracy* (Baton Rouge: Louisiana State University Press, 1993), 154–56; Richmond *Constitutional Whig,* Aug. 29, 1831. Jordan, after examining all extant issues of the Richmond *Enquirer* for August and September, 1831, found not even any intimation of rape on the part of Turner's rebels. Nor were there any hints of rape in such newspapers as the Boston *Columbian Sentinel,* the Albany *Argus,* the New York *Post,* the Harrisburg *Chronicle,* the Milledgeville *Federal Union,* or the Mobile *Register,* all of which quoted at length from Virginia newspapers. See also Robert N. Elliott,

"The Nat Turner Insurrection as Reported in the North Carolina Press," *North Carolina Historical Review* 38 (1961), 1–18.

58. Higginson, "Nat Turner's Insurrection," 175–77; Jordan, *Tumult and Silence*, 155. Walter White, in his 1929 study of lynching, reported that the issue of interracial sex was distorted by what he called a "conspiracy of semi-silence into an importance infinitely greater than the actual facts concerning it would justify." That silence, he said, was the result of a willful blindness to "the historical fact the rape of black women by white men during and after slavery," combined with what he called "a hallucinatory frenzy" about the craving for and rape of white women by black men, which, he said, "exists more in fantasy than in fact." That silence, he said, prevented many Southerners from any kind of response except one of "berserk rage." See Walter White, *Rope and Faggot: A Biography of Judge Lynch* (New York: Arno Press, 1969), 54–55.

59. Drewry, *Southampton Insurrection*, 117; Jordan, *Tumult and Silence*, 155–56.

60. *CONT,* 368; Gray, "Confessions," in *TBWR*, 105–106; Woodward and Lewis, "Confessions of William Styron," 89; Genovese, "William Styron before the People's Court," 204; Bennett, "Nat's Last White Man," *TBWR*, 15. See also Johnson, *Nat Turner Slave Insurrection*, 235–36. Styron said in a 1965 interview that "one of the things about this Negro, Nat Turner, is that he took it upon himself to do this incredible thing, to slaughter a lot of white people, which for an American Negro was probably the most prodigious and decisive act of free will ever taken." Nat Turner, he said, "couldn't deal with the violence that he himself had ordained, so to speak, and this is part of my story. I think it's very central to the book—the idea of what happens when a man boldly proposes a course of total annihilation and starts to carry it out and finds to his dismay that it's not working for him. I think it's unavoidable in an honest reading of Nat Turner's confessions that he himself was almost unable to grapple with violence, to carry it out successfully." According to Styron, "the Nat Turner I created (and perhaps the Nat Turner I believe might have existed), failed for the very reason of his humanity." See Jack Griffin, Jerry Hornsy, and Gene Stelzig, "A Conversation with William Styron," in *Pennsylvania Review* I (Spring, 1965), reprinted in *Conversations*, 57; Canzoneri and Stegner, "Interview with William Styron," 69; Ben Forkner and Gilbert Schricke, "An Interview with William Styron," *Conversations*, 194.

61. Bennett, "Nat's Last White Man," *TBWR*, 12, 15; J. Floyd to J. Hamilton, Jr., Nov. 19, 1831, in Duff and Mitchell, eds., *Nat Turner Rebellion*, 44; Higginson, "Nat Turner's Insurrection," 181; unsigned communication [presumably from Governor John Floyd] to *Richmond Whig*, Sept. 17, 1831, in Duff and Mitchell, eds., *Nat Turner Rebellion*, 35; Gray, "Confessions," in *TBWR*, 104, 115, 113.

62. Johnson, *Nat Turner Insurrection*, 235–36: J. Floyd to J. Hamilton, Jr., Nov. 19, 1831, in Duff and Mitchell, eds., *Nat Turner Rebellion*, 44.

63. Bennett, "Nat's Last White Man," *TBWR*, 7; Poussaint, "Dilemma of William Styron," *TBWR*, 17–18; Kaiser, "Failure of William Styron," *TBWR*, 63, 65; Killens, "Confessions of Willie Styron," *TBWR*, 36 passim. The contributors to *TBWR* misstate some facts, which it might be best to assume were consequences of zeal rather than malice: Styron's *Confessions* received neither unqualified praise from white reviewers nor unqualified opprobrium from black reviewers. Nor was their charge true that no blacks were invited to review Styron's *Confessions*.

64. Styron, introduction to *This Quiet Dust*, 6.

65. Vincent Harding, "You've Taken My Nat and Gone," *TBWR*, 29. Among the most significant collections and analyses of authentic field-recorded African-American folklore are Roger D. Abrahams, *Deep Down in the Jungle: Negro Narrative Folklore from the Streets of Philadelphia* (Hatboro, Pa.: Folklore Associates, 1964) and his "Trickster, the Outrageous Hero," in *Our Living Traditions* ed. Tristram Potter Coffin (New York: Basic Books, 1968); Roger Bastide, *African Civilisations in the New World*, trans. Peter Green (New York, 1971); J. Mason Brewer, *Humorous Tales of the South Carolina Negro* (Orangeburg: South Carolina State College, 1945); and his "John Tales," *Publications of the Texas Folklore Society* 21 (1946), 81–104; A[bigail]. M. H. Christensen, *Afro-American Folk Lore Told Round Cabin Fires in the Sea Islands of South Carolina* (Boston: J. P. Cupples, 1892); Daniel J. Crowley, ed., *African Folklore in the New World* (Austin: University of Texas Press, 1977); Richard M. Dorson, *American Negro Folk Tales* (Greenwich, Conn.: Fawcett, 1967); Alan Dundes, "African and Afro-American Tales," in *African Folklore* ed. Crowley, and his "African Tales among the North American Indians," *Southern Folklore Quarterly* 29 (1965), 207–19; Ambrose E. Gonzáles, *The Black Border: Gullah Stories of the Carolina Coast* (Columbia: The State Publishing Co., 1922); Zora Neale Hurston, "High John de Conquer," *American Mercury* 57 (1943), 450–58; and her *Mules and*

Men (Philadelphia: J. P. Lippincott, 1935); Bruce Jackson, ed., *The Negro and His Folklore in Nineteenth Century Periodicals* (Austin: University of Texas, 1967); Guy B. Johnson, *Folk Culture on St. Helena Island, South Carolina* (Chapel Hill: University of North Carolina Press, 1930); Charles Colcock Jones, Jr., *Negro Myths from the Georgia Coast* (Boston: Houghton-Mifflin Co., 1888); Lawrence W. Levine, *Black Culture and Black Consciousness; Afro-American Folk Thought from Slavery to Freedom* (New York: Oxford University Press, 1977), esp. pp. 81–135; Harry C. Oster, "Negro Humor: John and Old Marster," *Journal of the Folklore Institute* 5 (1968), 42–57; Elsie Clews Parsons, *Folk-Lore of the Antilles, French and English* (Cambridge: Harvard University Press, 1923), her *Folk-Lore of the Sea Islands, South Carolina* (Cambridge: Harvard University Press, 1923), and her *Folk-Tales of Andros Island, Bahamas* (Cambridge: Harvard University Press, 1918); *South Carolina Folk Tales*, compiled by Workers of the Writers' Program of the Work Projects Administration in the State of South Carolina (Columbia: University of South Carolina, 1941); and Sterling Stuckey, "Through the Prism of Folklore: The Black Ethos in Slavery," *Massachusetts Review* 9 (1968). According to Eugene D. Genovese, "there is little evidence of a revolutionary folk tradition among the southern slaves of the kind that Palmares inspired among the slaves of the Brazilian northeast." He believes that the reason "no powerful tradition emerged" was simply that neither the Turner rebellion nor such other revolts as the Stono Rebellion, Gabriel's Rebellion, or the Denmark Vesey Revolt ever "achieved an appropriate size or duration." See his *Roll, Jordan, Roll: The World the Slaves Made* (New York: Pantheon, 1974), 596–97.

66. Henry Clay Bruce, *The New Man: Twenty-Nine Years a Slave, Twenty Nine Years a Free Man: Recollections of H. C. Bruce* (York, Penn.: P. Anstadt and Sons, 1895), 25–26; Allen Crawford, North Emporia, Va., interviewed by Susie R. C. Byrd, June 25, 1937, in Charles L. Perdue, Jr., Thomas E. Barden, and Robert K. Phillips, *Weevils in the Wheat: Interviews with Virginia Ex-Slaves* (Charlottesville: University Press of Virginia, 1976), 75–76. Cf. Gray, "Confessions," *TBWR*, 105–108.

67. Fannie Berry, Petersburg, Va., interviewed by Susie R. C. Byrd, February 26, 1937, in Perdue, *Weevils in the Wheat*, 35; Linda Brent [Harriet Jacobs], *Incidents in the Life of a Slave Girl*, ed. Lydia Maria Child (Boston: author, 1861), p. 102. The standard modern edition is Harriet Jacobs, *Incidents in the Life of a Slave Girl*, ed. Jean Fagan Yellin (Cambridge: Harvard University Press, 1987).

68. Charity Bowery, interviewed by Lydia Maria Child, in her "Charity Bowery," *The Liberty Bell: By Friends of Freedom*, ed. Maria W. Chapman (Boston: American Anti-Slavery Society, 1839), 42–43; James Lindsay Smith, *Autobiography of James Lindsay Smith, including, also, Reminiscences of Slave Life, Recollections of the War, Education of Freedmen, Causes of the Exodus, etc.* (Norwich: Press of the Bulletin, 1881), 162–65.

69. Jacobs, *Incidents in the Life of a Slave Girl*, 98–99; Allen Crawford, in Perdue, *Weevils in the Wheat*, 75–76; Henry Box Brown, *Narrative of the Life Henry Box Brown, Written by Himself* (Boston: Samuel Webb, 1852) 19; Jacobs, *Incidents in the Life of a Slave Girl*, 102.

70. Allen Crawford, in Perdue, *Weevils in the Wheat*, 75–76.

71. Bowery interviewed by Lydia Maria Child, 42; Jamie Parker, *Jamie Parker, the Fugitive; Related to Mrs. Emily Pierson* (Hartford: Brockett, Fuller, and Co., 1851), 16–17.

72. "The real Nat Turner as opposed to the one I created were and are two different people," Styron acknowledged to an interviewer in 1974. See Ben Forkner and Gilbert Schricke, "An Interview with William Styron," *Southern Review* 10 (1974), 923–34, reprinted in *Conversations*, 192–93.

73. Peter Nicholas Corodimas, "Guilt and Redemption in the Novels of William Styron" (Ph.D. diss., Ohio State University, 1971); Ardner Randolph Cheshire, Jr., "The Theme of Redemption in the Fiction of William Styron" (Ph.D. diss., Louisiana State University, 1973). An earlier study, Jonathan Baumbach's "The Theme of Guilt and Redemption in the Post Second World War Novel" (Ph.D. diss., Stanford University, 1961) points to themes of guilt and redemption in Styron's *Lie Down in Darkness* along with selected works by Saul Bellow, Ralph Ellison, Bernard Malamud, Wright Morris, Flannery O'Connor, J. D. Salinger, and Robert Penn Warren. Styron concedes that "the themes of all my books do somehow revolve around the idea that people act out of selfish and willful and prideful motivations without realizing that the universe is fairly indifferent and doesn't care, and that more often than not these willful acts will result in some kind of catastrophe, especially if they're directed in terms of violence against other people." See Forkner and Schricke, "Interview with William Styron," *Conversations*, 191.

74. William Styron, *The Long March* (New York: Random House, 1952); William Styron, *Set This House on Fire* (New York: Random House, 1960). "Mannix was a total figment of my imagination,"

Styron told an interviewer in 1977. "That part did not really happen. Nor did he really exist." See Michael West, "An Interview with William Styron," in *Conversations*, 223. Kinsolving's affinity for alcohol may be semiautobiographical. Styron denies ever having written a line under the influence of alcohol, but says that having "a few drinks" allows the writer "to think in this released mode" in a way that "often gives you very new insights" and "certain visionary moments" that are "very valuable." See Hilary Mills, "Creators on Creating: William Styron," in *Conversations*, 241. Styron's indebtedness to theologian Paul Tillich is stressed by Rohart Detweiler in his "William Styron and the Courage to Be," in *Four Spiritual Crises in Mid-Century American Fiction* (Gainesville: University Press of Florida, 1964), 6–13. Nancy Carter Goodley emphasizes the influence of Christian existentialist Soren Kierkegaard on what she calls the "strongly affirmative and Christian" theology of Styron's work in her "All Flesh is Grass: Despair and Affirmation in *Lie Down in Darkness*, (Ph.D. diss., American University, 1975).

75. William Styron, *Lie Down in Darkness* (Indianapolis: Bobbs-Merrill, 1951). Styron recalled in an interview that "if that final monologue of Peyton has any intensity, it might be due to the fact that I was monstrously oppressed" at the time by what he was certain would be a bad time. He had been called up for active duty in the U.S. Marine Corps. He had served two and a half years during the second World War and had remained in the Reserves. "I was called up in 1951 at the very height of the Korean War. I was just finishing *Lie Down in Darkness*, and I was working against time because I wanted to get the thing done before I went back in to the marines." See Griffin, Hornsy, and Stelzig, "Conversation with William Styron," in *Conversations*, 52.

76. Styron, *Lie Down in Darkness*, 394–95.

77. According to the Ten, "Styron's selection of 'factual' and psychological material speaks for itself." Of course. So does it for all writers, whether of fiction or fact, not excluding the Ten Black Writers themselves. Bennett, "Nat's Last White Man," *TBWR*, 4; Kaiser, "Failure of William Styron," *TBWR*, 64. Eudora Welty, *One Writer's Beginnings* (Cambridge: Harvard University Press, 1983), 110–11; Poussaint, "Dilemma of William Styron," *TBWR*, 21; Forkner and Schricke, "Interview with William Styron," 192–93; Meras, "Interviews William Styron," 30. Welty—writing of Miss Eckhart, the piano teacher in her *The Golden Apples*—adds that "there wasn't any resemblance in her outward identity," Welty notes carefully. "What ani-

mates and possesses me is what drives Miss Eckhart, the love of her art and the love of giving it, the desire to give it until there is no more left." It was not in the character "as she stands solidly and almost opaquely in the surround of her story, but in the making of her character out of my most inward and most deeply feeling self, I would say I have found my voice in my fiction" (*One Writer's Beginnings,* 111).

78. William Styron, "Jimmy in the House," *New York Times Book Review,* Dec. 20, 1987, 30.

79. James Baldwin, *Go Tell It On the Mountain* (New York: Alfred A. Knopf, 1953), 27; James Baldwin, "Everybody's Protest Novel," in his *Notes of a Native Son* (Boston: Beacon Press, 1955; reprint 1964), 21.

80. Baldwin, *Go Tell It On the Mountain,* 228.

81. James Baldwin, *Another Country* (New York: Dial Press, 1962), 22.

82. Baldwin, "Everybody's Protest Novel," 13–23; Styron, "Jimmy in the House," 30.

83. Richard Wright, *Native Son* (New York, 1940), 17, 101; James Baldwin, "Many Thousands Gone," in *Notes of a Native Son,* 29.

84. *CONT,* 172 , 349 , 255–56 .

85. Baldwin, *Another Country,* 22; Wright, *Native Son,* 81–85, 108; Eldridge Cleaver, *Soul on Ice* (New York: McGraw-Hill, 1968), 14.

86. Wright, *Native Son,* 108–109, 101.

87. Ralph Ellison, *Invisible Man* (New York: Random House, 1952), 7–8.

88. Herman Melville, "Benito Cereno," in his *Piazza Tales* (New York: Dix and Edwards, 1856). "Benito Cereno" is based on an actual slave mutiny that took place on board a Spanish ship off South America in 1799.

89. Harriet Beecher Stowe, *Dred: A Tale of the Great Dismal Swamp* (Boston: Phillips, Sampson, and Co., 1856). *Dred* is less concerned with the black rebel of the dismal swamp than with the interlocking relationships among an interracial family, like that of Thomas Sutpen in Faulkner's *Absalom, Absalom!* According to Higginson, "Mrs. Stowe's 'Dred' seems dim and melodramatic beside the actual Nat Turner." See his "Nat Turner's Insurrection," 209.

90. Arna Bontemps, *Black Thunder* (New York: Macmillan, 1936), 82. As a matter of fact, Styron had planned to write his Nat Turner novel "from an omniscient point of view, from many reactive standpoints, such as that of one of the white victims, one of the

farmer types." But "it just didn't seem right to me," and he eventually realized that he would have to "risk leaping into a black man's consciousness. Not only did I want the risk alone—which was an important thing, to see if it could be done—but by doing so, I thought I could get a closer awareness of the smell of slavery." Filtering through "the consciousness of the 'I', the first person," he hoped, "would somehow allow you to enter the consciousness of a Negro of the early decades of the nineteenth century." He added that "if you start finding out about Nat, discovering things about Nat, well, of course, every passage, every chapter, every section is kind of a revelation both for yourself and for Nat." See Canzoneri and Stegner, "Interview with William Styron," *Conversations*, 69–70, and Brazelan and Sussman, "William Styron on *The Confessions of Nat Turner*," *Conversations*, 103.

91. Styron, *This Quiet Dust*, 247. Of course, the Faulkner influence on Styron, as on virtually all Southern writers, is palpable—as both god and demon. "Writers as disparate as Flannery O'Connor and Walker Percy have expressed their despair at laboring in the shadow of such a colossus," Styron has written, "and I felt a similar measliness (*This Quiet Dust*, 292)." It is interesting to ponder how Nat Turner might have fared in Faulkner's hands. John A. Williams suggests that he might well have resembled the cold, unremitting Lucas Beauchamp of *Go Down, Moses* and *Intruder In the Dust*. See Williams, "The Manipulation of History," in *TBWR*, 48.

92. See F. Garvin Davenport, Jr., *The Myth of Southern History: Historical Consciousness in Twentieth Century Southern Literature* (Nashville: Vanderbilt University Press, 1970), 131–70; Richard H. King, *A Southern Renaissance: The Cultural Awakening of the American South, 1930–1955* (New York: Oxford University Press, 1980), 72–76, 231–41, 277–86; Daniel Joseph Singal, *The War Within: From Victorian to Modernist Thought in the South, 1919–1945* (Chapel Hill: University of North Carolina Press, 1982), 339–72; C. Vann Woodward, "History in Robert Penn Warren's Fiction," in his *The Future of the Past*, 221–34.

93. Peter H. Wood, "Nat Turner: the Unknown Slave as Visionary Leader," in *Black Leaders of the Nineteenth Century*, in eds. Leon Litwack and August Meier (Urbana: 1988), 37–39.

94. Styron, *This Quiet Dust*, 9–34. The quotes are on pp. 10, 12, 11, 14. The essay, "This Quiet Dust," was originally published in *Harper's*, Apr., 1965; Granville Hicks, "Race Riot, 1831," *Saturday Review*, Oct. 7, 1967.

95. Ellison et al., "The Uses of History in Fiction," *Conversations,* 128, 130, 142; C. Vann Woodward, "Fictional History and Historical Fiction," *New York Review of Books,* Nov. 16, 1987, 38. According to Roland Barthes, "myth is constituted by the loss of the historical reality of things: in it, things lose the memory that they once were made." See his *Mythologies* (London: Paladin, 1973), 134–42. The quotation is on p. 155. See also Tony Bennett, "Text, Readers, Reading Formations," *Literature and History* 9 (1983).

96. Ralph Ellison, "Twentieth Century Fiction and the Black Mask of Humanity," in his *Shadow and Act* (New York: Random House, 1953), 42–43; Willie Lee Rose, *Slavery and Freedom* (New York: Random House, 1982), 169; Ellison, *The Invisible Man.*

97. Ellison, "Twentieth-Century Fiction," in *Shadow and Act,* 43; Kaiser, "Failure of William Styron," *TBWR,* 56; Killens, "Confessions of Willie Styron," *TBWR,* 36; Genovese, "William Styron before the People's Court," 203–204. Genovese points out that the novelist's depiction of Nat Turner shared many characteristics with the historical Toussaint L'Ouverture, the successful black revolutionary of Saint Domingue. A "privileged" bondsman, Toussaint led his own master's family to safety, remained aloof from the violence while his fellow slaves put the North Plain to the torch. "Not being a statue," he writes, Toussaint possessed "all the frailties and contradictions common even to the greatest of men" (204–205).

98. Styron, *This Quiet Dust,* 13; Ralph Ellison, introduction to *Shadow and Act,* xi–xxiii; Meras, "Interviews William Styron," 30; Richard Wright, *White Man, Listen!* (New York: Doubleday, 1957), 108–109 (emphasis mine).

99. Toni Morrison, *Playing in the Dark: Whiteness and the Literary Imagination* (Cambridge: Harvard University Press, 1992), 11–12; James Baldwin, "Many Thousands Gone," *Partisan Rev{{idotless}}ew* 18 (1951), 673–74; William Faulkner, "A Letter to the Leaders of the Negro Race," in his *Essays, Speeches and Public Letters,* ed. James B. Meriwether (New York: Random House, 1956), 110.

100. According to Styron, while writing the *Confessions,* he came to realize that his protagonist was "ignorant of his own pride, was ignorant of his own undertaking, was ignorant of the enormity of what he was doing—mainly this horrible act of violence in the name of retribution which—well meant or not—resulted in catastrophe, not only for himself and of course the white people, but especially for his own people, the blacks." See Forkner and Schricke, "Interview

with William Styron," *Conversations,* 191. Such unrecognized overweening pride is, of course, what Aristotle called the "tragic flaw" in his *Poetics.*

101. Joel Williamson, *The Crucible of Race: Black-White Relations in the American South Since Emancipation* (New York: Oxford University Press, 1984), 522.

Contributors

SUSAN A. EACKER holds a doctoral degree from Miami University, Oxford, Ohio. Her contribution to this volume won the 1994 Webb-Smith Essay Competition.

ANNE GOODWYN JONES is associate professor of English at the University of Florida. She is the author of *Tomorrow is Another Day: The Woman Writer in the South, 1859–1936* (1981) and *Theory and the Good Old Boys: Manhood and Writing in the Modern South* (forthcoming). She is at work on *Faulkner's Daughters*, a two-volume study of women writers of the Southern Renaissance.

CHARLES JOYNER is Burroughs Distinguished Professor of Southern History and Culture at the University of South Carolina, Coastal Carolina College. He is the author of *Down by the Riverside: A South Carolina Slave Community* (1984), *Remember Me: Slave Life in Coastal Georgia* (1989), and numerous other books and essays on Southern history, literature, and folklore.

CHRISTOPHER MORRIS is assistant professor of history at the University of Texas at Arlington. He is the author of *Becoming Southern: The Evolution of a Way of Life, Warren County and Vicksburg, Mississippi 1770–1860* (1995).

MICHAEL O'BRIEN is Phillip R. Shriver Professor of History at Miami University. He is the author of *Rethinking the South: Es-*

says in *Intellectual History, The Idea of the American South, 1920–1941*, and *A Character of Hugh Legaré.*

STEVEN G. REINHARDT is associate professor of history at the University of Texas at Arlington. He is the author of *Justice in the Sarladais, 1770–1790,* and has published articles and reviews on crime and the criminal justice system in early modern France in the *Journal of Interdisciplinary History* and *European History Quarterly.* He is also chair of the Webb lectures committee.

BERTRAM WYATT-BROWN is Richard J. Milbauer Professor of History at the University of Florida. He is the author of *Southern Honor: Ethics and Behavior in the Old South* (1982), *Yankee Saints and Southern Sinners* (1985), *The Literary Percys: Family History, Gender, and the Southern Imagination* (1994), and *The House of Percy: Honor, Melancholy, and Imagination in a Southern Family* (1994).